Anonymous

Memorial Of The Twenty-Fifth Anniversary Of The Consecration Of
The Most Rev. John J. Williams, Archbishop of Boston

Anonymous

Memorial Of The Twenty-Fifth Anniversary Of The Consecration Of The Most Rev. John J. Williams, Archbishop of Boston

ISBN/EAN: 9783744653442

Printed in Europe, USA, Canada, Australia, Japan

Cover: Foto ©ninafisch / pixelio.de

More available books at **www.hansebooks.com**

MEMORIAL

OF THE

TWENTY-FIFTH ANNIVERSARY

OF THE CONSECRATION OF

THE MOST REV. JOHN J. WILLIAMS, D. D.,

ARCHBISHOP OF BOSTON,

ON

THURSDAY, MARCH 12, 1891.

BERNARD CORR, Editor.

BOSTON:
JAMES L. CORR & CO., PUBLISHERS,
286 WASHINGTON STREET.
1891.

CONTENTS.

CATHOLICITY IN BOSTON.

		PAGES.
PART I.	Events from 1630 to 1788 Penal Laws. Catholic Missionaries in America. Visit of Father Druilletes to Boston. First Recognition of Catholicity. Washington's Order. French Fleet in Boston Harbor. Visit of Abbe Robin.	7—12
PART II.	From 1788 to 1792. Abbe Poterie. First Priest stationed in Boston. First Public Mass. First Catholic Church in School Street. "Church of the Holy Cross." Rev. John Thayer. Full Account of his Conversion.	13—20
PART III.	From 1792 to 1823. Arrival of Rev. F. Matignon. Departure of Father Thayer to Kentucky. His Death in Ireland. Arrival of Rev. John L. de Cheverus. His Missionary Labors. Purchase of Franklin Street Lot. Subscribers to the New Church of the Holy Cross. Its Dedication. Gift of the Bell. Consecration of Bishop Cheverus. First Bishop of Boston. Death of Dr. Matignon. Departure of Bishop Cheverus. The Ursuline Nuns.	21—32
PART IV.	From 1823 to 1846 Arrival of Bishop Fenwick. Very Rev. Wm. Taylor. Clergymen with Bishop Fenwick. His Diocese. Enlargement of the Holy Cross Cathedral. Ordination of Fathers Fitton and Wiley. Destruction of Ursuline Convent. New Churches. St. Vincent's Orphan Asylum. Worcester College. Death of Bishop Fenwick.	33—39
PART V.	From 1846 to 1866. Bishop Fitzpatrick. His Parents and Public School Education. His Ordination and Consecration. Fruits of his Labors. Last Days of the Franklin Street Cathedral. Rev. James A. Healy's Discourse. Removal to Castle Street. Death of Bishop Fitzpatrick. List of Clergymen attached to Cathedral.	37—43
PART VI	Archbishop Williams. His Birth and Parentage. His First Schooling. His Education in Montreal and Paris. His Ordination. His Labors as a Priest. His Consecration. Building of the New Cathedral. Father Lyndon. Principal Subscribers. Boston Raised to an Archdiocese. Investiture of the Pallium. Dedication of the Cathedral. Progress of Catholicity. Charitable and Educational Institutions. Catholic Churches and Clergymen in Boston. Description of New Cathedral.	44—62

SILVER JUBILEE OF THE CONSECRATION OF ARCHBISHOP WILLIAMS.

PAGES.

PONTIFICAL MASS IN THE CATHEDRAL. Sermon of Bishop Healy.
Prelates and Clergymen Present. The Music. 63—78

BANQUET IN HONOR OF THE ARCHBISHOP.

Address of the Clergy. Toasts. Responses. Presentations. 79—88

RECEPTION BY THE CATHOLIC UNION.

Addresses of President Thos. B. Fitz and Hon. Thomas J. Gargan.
Reply of the Archbishop. Mrs. Blake's Jubilee Ode.
Names of Bishops and Clergymen Present. Names of Members. 89—118

ST. JAMES PARISIONERS.

Address and Presentation. 119—123

NOTRE DAME ACADEMY.

Reception by Pupils of the Archdiocese. Salutatory. Addresses. Response of the Archbishop. The Sisters' Present. Historical. 125—136

SACRED HEART ACADEMY.

Reception. Addresses and Presentations. 137—138

ST. VINCENT DE PAUL SOCIETY,

Extraordinary General Meeting. Congratulatory Address. Speeches.
Reply of the Archbishop. 139—148

CARMELITE NUNS.

A Visit to the Nunnery. 149—151

THE STUDENTS' GIFT.

From Students in St. John's Seminary. 151

A CARD.

Acknowledgments of the Catholic Union. 152

ADVERTISEMENTS.

	PAGES.
COLE & WOODBERRY,	
Church Organs.	153
FLYNN & MAHONY,	
Catholic Publishers, Church Goods, etc.	153
EMERSON PIANO COMPANY,	
Pianos.	154
McDONNELL & SONS,	
Quincy Granite, Monuments, etc.	155
THEIS & JANSSEN,	
Ecclesiastical and Architectural Marble Works, etc.	156
JOSEPH SIBBEL,	
Modeller and Sculptor.	156
NICHOLAS M. WILLIAMS,	
Funeral Director and Undertaker.	156
MAYER & CO.,	
Stained Glass, Statues, etc.	157
JOHN CONLON & CO.,	
Altar Wines, etc.,	158
A. ERTLE,	
Church Decorator, etc.	158
UNION INSTITUTION FOR SAVINGS,	
Hugh O'Brien, President; Wm. S. Pelletier, Treasurer.	158
JAMES L. CORR & CO.,	
Printers, etc.	159

ACKNOWLEDGMENTS.

In the preparation of the historical sketch, the following authorities have been consulted:—History of New England, Boston Town Records, De Lorgues' Life of Columbus, Rev. John Thayer's Autobiography, Father Fitton's History of the Catholic Church in New England, Rev. A. S. Healy's Sketch of Catholicity in Boston, O'Kane Murray's History of the Catholic Church in America, American Historical Magazine, Drake's History of Boston, Shurtleff's Landmarks of Boston, and old Boston Directories.

For information and suggestions the editor is under obligations to Most Rev. John J. Williams, Right Rev. James A. Healy, Very Rev. Wm. Byrne, Rev. R. Neagle, Dr. Hasket Derby, and Mr. Patrick Donahoe.

B. C.

BOSTON, April 25, 1891.

CATHOLICITY IN BOSTON.

PART I.

Events from 1630 to 1788.

The Catholic Church held no position in Boston during the period of one hundred and fifty-eight years, from the landing of the Puritans in 1630 till after the adoption of the Constitution in 1788. The early settlers from England, though possessing many noble traits, brought with them an intense hatred of Catholicity and everything pertaining to it. They came to establish civil and religious liberty for themselves, but denied it to all others who differed from their narrow Calvinistic creed.

Here they attempted to build up a Church and State, and passed an order in 1631, "that for the time to come none should be admitted to the freedom of the body politic, but such as were church members." In 1664, they relaxed so far as to allow freeholders rated at ten shillings, and certified by the minister to be "Orthodox in their principles" to be freemen, though not church members. Besides "Papists," this excluded Baptists, Quakers, Episcopalians, and Independent Protestants like Roger Williams. The penal laws of England were strictly enforced, and anybody suspected of "Papacy" was treated as a criminal.

In 1692, when the two Massachusetts Colonies were erected into a single Royal Province, under a new charter from William and Mary, liberty of conscience was assured to all but Catholics. The Episcopal form of worship was placed upon the same footing as the Congregational, and church membership was no longer to be a qualification for citizenship. Still, the prejudice against Catholics remained as strong as ever, and the Mother Church had no recognition. The witchcraft mania which raged before and about this time was made a source of persecution to anybody suspected of "Papist" tendencies. One of its earliest victims was a woman known as Goody Glover, and supposed to be a Catholic from Ireland. Father Fitton, in his valuable "Sketches of the Establishment of the Church in New England," gives the following interesting account of this woman:—

"Mrs. Glover, for such was her name, was probably one of the unfortunate women whom English barbarity tore from their homes in Ireland to sell as slaves in America. English she could scarcely speak; and, on being accused as a witch, by a certain Miss Goodwin, for whom her daughter worked, she was arrested and put to the usual tests, one of which was the repetition of the Lord's Prayer; she repeated it in Irish, but as it was not understood, they required more. She repeated it next in Latin, but not quite correctly; in English, she could not, as she had never learned it. This, however, corroborated the testimony of the girl, her accuser, and the poor Irish woman was hanged, because she could not pray in a language to her foreign and unknown, and, strangely enough, for not praying in pure Latin!"

Notwithstanding all the restrictions and persecutions, a few Catholics from time to time found their way to Boston and quietly lived here without any profession of faith. Soon after its settlement, Boston became the most important seaport of the Colonies and it carried on a flourishing trade with England, the West Indies, and other ports in America. From a volume of the "Boston Town Records," under date of September 22, 1746, the following has been copied:—

"Whereas it is suggested that there are several persons Roman Catholicks that now dwell and reside in this Town and it may be very Dangerous to permit such persons to Reside here in Case we should be attack'd by an Enemy, Therefore Voted that Mr. Jeremiah Allen Mr. Nathaniel Gardner and Mr. Joseph Bradford be and hereby are appointed a Committee to take Care and prevent any Danger the Town may be in from Roman Catholicks residing here by making Strict Search and enquiry after all such and pursue such methods relating to em as the Law directs."

On the 25th of September, the "Town mett according to Adjournment" and "The Committee appointed the 22d instant to take Care and prevent any Danger the Town may be in by Roman Catholicks residing here, Reported that they had found the Laws now in force relating to such persons to be insufficient To Enable them to Effect the same and therefore could do nothing hereon altho they suspected a considerable number of Roman Catholicks to be now in Town, —— Whereupon it was moved & Voted that the Representatives of this Town be and hereby are desired to Endeavour at the next Session of the General Court to get a Law pass'd that shall be effectual to Secure the Town from any Danger they may be in, by Roman Catholicks Dwelling here."

While the Catholic religion was barred out of Massachusetts in Colonial days, it was steadily spreading in other parts of the New World. In the North under the protection of the French flag, the heroic Jesuit Missionaries were converting the Indians in the forests of Maine, along the banks of the St. Lawrence, and on the shores of the Great Lakes. In the South, the zealous English Jesuit Fathers White and Altham, who landed with the Catholic Pilgrims on the shores of Maryland in 1634, labored successfully among the Indians and Colonists; and the enterprising Franciscan and Dominican Fathers carried the blessings of Christian civilization farther South, from Florida to the shores of the Pacific. To Massachusetts must be accorded the discredit of resisting the establishment of the Catholic Church long after it had gained a foothold in almost every other place in America.

As early as 1650, only twenty years after the settlement of Boston, the Rev. Gabriel Druillettes, the Jesuit Apostle of Maine, visited the Puritan town, on the invitation and under the protection of the authorities. He came as a plenipotentiary to confer with Governor Dudley and other commissioners about joining an alliance with the Abnaki Indians in Maine. He reached Boston on the Feast of the Immaculate Conception, 1650, and was graciously received by the officials. "The principal men of Charlestown," writes Father Fitton, "immediatelely waited on him, and Major-General Gibbons, being informed of the character in which he came, invited him to his house." In his own narrative, the good Jesuit Father says:—

"He [Gibbons] gave the key of a room where I might, in all liberty, pray, and perform the other exercises of my religion; and he besought me to take no other lodging while I was in Boston."

Father Druillettes does not state that he carried his missionary chalice with him; "but," Father Fitton says, "as this is by no means improbable, we may infer that the Holy Sacrifice of the Mass was offered in Boston, in December, 1650."

In regard to the movements of Father Druillettes, Rev. Mr. Fitton gives the following interesting account:—

"He began his negotiations with Governor Dudley and the Boston magistrates, but as the Abnakis lay in a territory claimed by Plymouth, they referred him to that Colony. The missionary accordingly started on the 21st of December for Plymouth. On his arrival there, he was very courteously received by Governor Bradford, who invited him to dinner, and very considerately had a dish of fish prepared, as it was Friday. The Plymouth people, more interested in the French trade than others, readily consented to give the aid which the Governor of Canada asked against the Iroquois as a condition of an alliance.

"Returning to Boston, he stopped on the way at Roxbury, and spent a night with the Protestant minister, John Eliot, the celebrated Apostle of the Indians. Here, too, he won esteem, and the New England missionary urged his French fellow-laborer to pass the winter with him. At Boston, Fr. Druillettes found the officials more inclined to aid the French, now that the Governor of Plymouth had expressed himself favorable, and having, by conferences and visits, gained all whom he could to vote in his favor at the next meeting of the commissioners, he sailed from Boston on the 3d of January, 1651, and putting into Marblehead on the 9th, left a proxy with Mr. Endicott, to act for him at the next meeting."

After the departure of Father Druillettes, nothing definite can be found of the visit of any Catholic clergymen to Boston until the Revolution. Mention is made of two French priests passing through the city on their way to France between 1687 and 1690, one of whom, Rev. Louis Petit, being carried off as a prisoner from Port Royal, Nova Scotia, during an assault made by the English under Sir Wm. Phips on the Acadian settlements.

In 1700, a new act was passed by Massachusetts, condemning Catholic missionaries to imprisonment and death if captured on her soil, charging them with all sorts of crimes. Under laws of this nature, the Catholic missionaries were forced to confine themselves to other parts of America. It was not until the Colonies threw off the yoke of England and declared themselves free and independent, that Catholic priests were tolerated in Boston.

To the illustrious Washington are Catholics indebted for the first favorable recognition. When he assumed command of the army around Boston in 1775, he was astonished to find that preparations were in progress to celebrate "Gun Powder Plot," by the usual custom of burning the Pope in effigy. He determined to stop the bigoted practice, so far as the camp was concerned, and issued the following order:—

"November 5th. As the Commander-in-chief has been apprised of a design formed for the observance of that ridiculous and childish custom of burning the effigy of the Pope, he cannot help expressing his surprise that there should be officers and soldiers in this army so void of common sense, as not to see the impropriety of such a step. * * * It is so monstrous as not to be suffered or excused; indeed, instead of offering the most remote insult, it is our duty to address public thanks to our (Catholic) brethren, as to them we are indebted for every late success over the common enemy in Canada."

The presence of the French fleet and armies in Boston Harbor, in 1778, under the command of the distinguished Count D'Estaing, was the occasion of the first public demonstration of Catholicity in the city of the Puritans. From the 25th of August till November, the fleet remained in the harbor, and the officers, most of whom were Catholics, were hospitably entertained by the citizens. Divine service was regularly performed on the vessels, and witnessed by many of the inhabitants, who were deeply impressed with the piety and respect of the crews. One of the French officers having died, the body was buried with all the impressive ceremonies of the church. The funeral was preceded by a large crucifix, and the members of the Town Council marched in the funeral procession through the streets of the city. What a gratifying sight this must have been for the few despised Catholics who had, at this time, made Boston their home!

Abbe Robin, who visited Boston as a chaplain in Count Rochambeau's fleet, wrote an interesting and intelligent description of Boston in 1781, in a series of letters to a friend. He gave the Bostonians the credit of observing the Sunday with "the utmost strictness, the most innocent recreations and pleasures being prohibited." In noticing the Protestant places of worship, he speaks approvingly of the order and respect observed by the congregations, but evidently was not pleased with the interior of the buildings. "All these churches are destitute of ornament," he said; "no addresses are made to the heart and the imagination; there is no visible object to suggest to the mind for what purpose a man comes into these places, who he is, and what he shortly will be. * * * The pomp of ceremony is here wanting to shadow out the greatness of the Being he goes to worship; there are no processions to testify the homage to Him, the Great Spirit of the Universe."

The Abbe no doubt missed the grand churches and ceremonies of his native France, and found nothing in Boston to satisfy his Catholic heart. He makes no mention of meeting any Catholics here, nor of exercising any religious functions.

PART II.

EVENTS FROM 1788 TO 1792.

The first Catholic clergyman stationed in Boston was Abbe CLAUDE FLORENT BOUCHARD DE LA POTERIE, a Frenchman, who had been a chaplain in the French fleet. Mention is made of the Abbe coming to Boston in 1784, but there is no account of his being authorized to perform the sacred functions till late in the year 1788. His first mass was celebrated in the house of a Mr. Baury, on Green Street, according to Rev. A. Sherwood Healy's interesting sketch of the Cathedral of Boston; but the old Huguenot church on School Street, having been secured by the few French, Spanish and Irish Catholics here, the first public mass was celebrated therein on Sunday, November 2, 1788. This building was named the "Church of the Holy Cross" by the Abbe, a title of singular appropriateness, in view of the fact that Columbus styled the New World the "Land of the Holy Cross." Little did sturdy John Endicott think, when he cut the cross out of the English flag because it was an emblem of "Popery," that the Holy Cross would be thus honored and perpetuated after that flag had been driven from the Colonies.

A memorandum of the Protestant Minister, Dr. Belknap, under date of November, 1788, says:—"The first Sabbath in this month, a Popish Chapel was opened in this town; the old French Protestant Meeting-house in School Street. A clergyman who was dismissed from the French fleet in disgrace officiates." Dr. Carroll, of Baltimore, who was then Prefect Apostolic of the Catholic Church in the United States, and who gave Abbe Poterie authority to officiate in Boston, evidently was not acquainted with the real character and standing of the Abbe, for in a few months afterwards, when information was received from France, the Abbe was summarily suspended, Rev. William O'Brien being sent from New York for that purpose. As soon as the church was opened, the French members of the little congregation sent an appeal to the Archbishop of Paris for "the necessary vestments and plate for the altar," which His Grace sent, with a portrait of himself, and a letter telling them to beware of a certain Abbe Poterie who was somewhere in America. The Abbe acknowledged that he was the person referred to, and left Boston when suspended by order of Dr. Carroll. The altar plate is still used in the Cathedral, and the picture of Mgr. de Juignez, the Archbishop, is now in the parlor of the episcopal residence.

With the Abbe, it seems, was associated Rev. L. ROUSSELET. Both clergymen were succeeded by Rev. JOHN THAYER, who was regularly appointed by Dr. Carroll to take charge of the New England mission. Perhaps the establishment of the Catholic Church in Boston should date from the appointment of Father Thayer, who began his pastorate on the 10th of June, 1790. He certainly appears to have been providentially prepared for this work. He was born in Boston, of a family in good circumstances, and brought up as a strict Protestant. He was educated for the ministry and performed its functions for two years in Boston. These facts and the following account of his conversion to the Catholic faith are taken from a book entitled "The Conversion of the Reverend John Thayer of Boston," written by himself, and published in Paris, in 1788.

Feeling a secret inclination to travel and learn the European languages, and acquire a knowledge of the customs, laws and governments of the principal nations, he started for France. "Such were my human views," he says, "without the least suspicion of the secret design of Providence, which was preparing me for more precious advantages."

He arrived in France at the end of the year 1781, and remained there ten months, studying the language and instructing himself in the principles of government. He was taken ill, and as he feared his sickness would be attended with serious consequences, his first concern was to forbid that any Catholic priest should come near him. After his recovery he spent three months in England, observing the manners and customs of the country. He returned to France, with the intention of passing to Rome. In his passage from Marseilles to Rome, the vessel was becalmed and obliged to stop several days at a little port called Port Ercole. He was entertained there by the Marquis D'Elmoro, the leading official of the place and a Catholic, " without any recommendations, with the kindness and affection of a father. Such goodness and cordiality to a stranger, to an avowed Protestant, touched and surprised me," says he. "This religion is not, then, so unsociable, and does not, as I have been told, inspire sentiments of aversion and intolerance to those of a different persuasion."

When he reached Rome, his first concern was to visit the most celebrated masterpieces and monuments of antiquity. While visiting the Pantheon, which formerly was a pagan temple, but now dedicated to the Blessed Virgin, he was led to respect the Church through whose power the cross of Jesus Christ was raised on wrecks of the idols. He soon acquired a knowledge of the Italian language, and was able to read its best authors. Being desirous of instructing himself thoroughly in the Catholic religion, for the same reason that he should have wished to know the religion of Mohammed if at Constantinople, he became desirous of knowing the doctrine of Catholics from their own lips.

"After having sought for an opportunity of conversing with some person well informed, both able and willing to instruct me thoroughly in the Catholic doctrines," says he, "I met with two ecclesiastics in a place which I was accustomed to frequent. I entered into conversation with them, and declared who I was and what I wanted. At that time I thought with respect to the Jesuits as all other Protestants do; but yet, I told them I should be glad to form an acquaintance with some of them. I know, said I, that they are cunning designing men, but they are celebrated for their learning; and while I profit by their lights, I will carefully guard myself against their subtlety."

The two persons with whom he was then conversing told him they were members of the Society of Jesus, and although they would not undertake to give him the instructions he desired, they said they would refer him to an able man, who could satisfy his inquiries. They introduced him to one of their brethren, who was distinguished for his learning and piety. Mr. Thayer told this good Father, that possibly he might have conceived some false notions of the Catholic religion, as all the knowledge he had of it was taken from the report of its enemies. And if this was the case, he wished to be undeceived. " For," said he, " I would not entertain a prejudice against any person, not even against the devil. Yet, do not think of converting me, for certainly you will not succeed."

The Father received him with gentleness and affability, and consented to have some conferences on religion with him. These were continued at intervals for about three months. Mr. Thayer listened each time without interrupting his instructor, but on his return home, never failed to set down in writing the difficulties and arguments which seemed to combat each one of the dogmas and articles. Although not convinced, he noticed the wonderful harmony through the whole system of the Catholic religion, and the wisdom which seemed to have something divine. As this learned Father could give only a few leisure hours at intervals, Mr. Thayer had recourse to another Jesuit, who surprised Mr. Thayer by telling him to go and say the Lord's Prayer thrice, and return to him on a certain day. Mr. Thayer complied, and met the Jesuit on the day appointed. He proposed his difficulties under several heads, and the good Father pointed out to him where these questions were treated, and procured him books on those subjects. Mr. Thayer also consulted an Augustinian friar, who took particular pains to show him the difference between articles of faith and simply opinions which the Church permits to be treated, without either adopting or rejecting them. This distinction threw a new light on the subject, and contributed greatly to clear up his ideas.

His researches carried him further than he had designed, as he had at first intended only to form an exact knowledge of the Catholic doctrine. But he was brought to such a state that he discovered nothing in it but what was reasonable. Still the prejudices in which he had been educated had too much influence over his mind, and his heart was not yet disposed to make the sacrifice which a profession of faith required. He was resolved, no matter what proof he received, not to change his religion while at Rome, for fear of taking a precipitate step. "But Providence," he says, " ever watchful over me, did not suffer these delays, which might have been fatal, but ordered various events which hastened my conversion." A work on the Guardian Angel, which he read at this time, made a great impression on him. He reproached himself for having too often failed in the respect which he owed to his Guardian Angel, and formed a resolution to be careful in future to avoid everything which could displease him. " This attention to preserve myself from sin," writes Mr. Thayer, " undoubtedly contributed to my conversion; at least, it removed an obstacle to the grace which God was about to bestow."

Such was his situation when the death of venerable Labre and the miracles which were performed through his intercession began to make a noise at Rome and to become the subject of every conversation. Notwithstanding the instructions which Mr. Thayer had received and the lights which he had acquired, he was nowise disposed to credit the public reports concerning this truly extraordinary person. Of all his prejudices against Catholics, the deepest rooted was a formal disbelief of miracles. Not content with denying those which were published at that time, he made them the subject of his raillery, and in the coffee-houses, passed some very unbecoming jests on the Servant of God. However, the number and weight of the evidences increasing daily, he thought it was his duty to examine the matter himself. He frequently conversed with the confessor of the deceased, from whom he learned a part of Blessed Labre's life. He visited four persons who were said to have been miraculously cured; he was convinced by his own eyes of the state in which they then were; he questioned them concerning the state in which they had been; he informed himself of the nature and continuance of the illness with which they had been attacked, and the circumstances of their cures which had been operated in an instant. After collecting full information he was convinced of the reality of each one of these miracles. Truth appeared to him on every side, but it was combatted by all the prejudices which he had imbibed from his infancy. He felt all the force of the arguments which Catholics oppose to the Protestant doctrine, but he had not the courage to yield. He clearly saw that he would be obliged to abjure the errors in which he had been brought up and which he had preached to others, and that he would be forced to renounce his ministry and his fortune. He was tenderly attached to his family, and he must incur their indignation. All these interests kept him back. "In a word," he says, "my understanding was convinced, but my heart was not changed."

He was in this fluctuating and undetermined state of mind when a little Italian book giving an account of the conversion of a Protestant Cavalier was put into his hands. When he received this book he had a secret presentiment that it would give him the finishing stroke, and it was with extreme difficulty that he could bring himself to read it. His soul was, as it were, rent by two contrary emotions, but at length the interests of eternal salvation prevailed. He threw himself on his knees and said a prayer, invoking the light of the Holy Ghost with the greatest possible sincerity. He then began to read and before he entirely finished the account, he exclaimed, "My God, I promise to become a Catholic!"

On the 25th of May, 1783, Mr. Thayer publicly abjured Protestantism, before a large assembly of former friends whom he had invited to the solemn ceremony. Having decided to embrace the ecclesiastical state for the greater glory of God and the salvation of his own soul as well as of those of his countrymen, he returned to France and entered the Seminary of St. Sulpice. After due preparation, he was ordained to the priesthood and returned to his native land.

Father Thayer reached Boston early in January, 1790, and was received with marked respect by his relatives and old friends. In a letter to a friend the following July he wrote: "On the first Sunday after my arrival I announced the word of God and all flocked in crowds to hear me. * * * About one hundred Catholics, consisting of French, Irishmen and Americans, are what constitute at present our church. About a dozen of them can attend mass daily." From this it appears that Father Thayer officiated with Abbe Poterie for a few months before the latter was suspended.

An interesting account of the first public mass celebrated by Father Thayer in Boston, is given by Mr. Samuel Breck, who became acquainted with Mr. Thayer in Paris, and, in fulfilment of a promise, assisted him in fitting up the chapel in Boston. "We fitted up a dilapidated and deserted meeting house in School Street, that was built in 1716, by some French Huguenots, * * * and now converted by us into a popish chapel. * * * Money was raised by subscription, with which the sacristy and vestry room was put in order; a pulpit was erected; the altar furnished; a few benches purchased for seats; and the little temple, which had served as a stable to the British in 1775, was once more consecrated to the uses of religion. The plate for the altar was borrowed of my father, and everything being made decent, the first public mass ever said in Boston was solemnized amid a large concourse of people of all persuasions. And this in a town where only thirteen years before the *Pope* and the *Devil*, were according to annual custom promenaded through the streets, on the 5th of November, in commemoration of the famous gunpowder plot; and, after serving as a spectacle of ridicule and scorn, were burnt together, leaving it doubtful in those days which of the two were the most hateful. I attended the mass, of course, and carried round the charity box as

Queteur." Mr. Breck wrote this some thirty years after the occurrence related, and probably had forgotten that other priests had preceded Father Thayer. The letter is published in "The American Catholic Historical Researches," of January, 1889. The statements in regard to the altar are also open to doubt.

PART III.

EVENTS FROM 1792 TO 1823.

After fighting for the faith single handed for about two years, the heart of our valiant American convert was made glad by the arrival of an assistant in the person of Rev. FRANCIS MATIGNON, Regius Professor of Divinity in the College of Navarre, who with other priests was exiled from their native France by the Revolution. Dr. Matignon was sent to Boston by Bishop Carroll, and he entered on the duties of his ministry on the 20th of August, 1792. He was received by Father Thayer "in his humble mansion as an angel from Heaven sent expressly to promote the great cause of the Redeemer by extending His Church in this section."

And a truly successful angel Dr. Matignon proved to be. He was 39 years of age and 14 years a priest, talented and pious, with a rich, vigorous imagination, a sound understanding, and a critical, profound learning. Born and educated in the centre of refinement, he was an accomplished gentleman, with a kindness of heart and delicacy of feeling which made him study the wants and anticipate the wishes of all he knew. He soon became aware of the bitter prejudices which existed in Boston against the Catholic Church, and of the foolish suspicions which the people entertained in regard to the designs of the Pope in sending such a highly cultured French clergyman to America. He found that the controversial discourses of Father Thayer had stirred up a strong feeling of opposition, and at first he was at a loss to know how to meet it. But he soon took in the situation and determined to master it. "With meekness and humility," says Father Fitton, "he disarmed the proud; with prudence, learning and ability he met the captious and slanderous; and so gentle and just was his course, that even the censorious forgot to watch him, and the malicious were too cunning to attack one armed so strong in his poverty."

When Dr. Matignon was fairly settled in Boston, Father Thayer felt at liberty, to extend his visits to other parts of New England. He made various excursions, and was able to remain for a time in places where his services were required. "In this way," says Father Fitton, "he continued to labor announcing the Gospel in every large town and village, and gaining many souls to God, by reclaiming them from heresy."

In 1799, Bishop Carroll, anxious to provide for the spiritual necessities of all confided to his pastoral care, withdrew Father Thayer from the New England mission, and sent him to labor in the state of Kentucky. While working on that mission, he conceived the design of establishing in his native city a convent school for young Catholic females. With the approbation of the Bishop, he left Kentucky, and went to Europe, with the view of raising funds for his cherished object. After collecting between eight and ten thousand dollars, Almighty God called the good priest from his earthly labors. He died in Limerick, Ireland, leaving his funds in trust to Dr. Matignon, for the purpose for which they were raised.

Before Father Thayer was transferred from the Boston mission, another able assistant arrived to take part in the good work. This was the learned and pious REV. JOHN LOUIS DE CHEVERUS, a native of Mayenne, France. He was an exile in England, teaching school, when Dr. Matignon, who knew him in Paris, urgently invited him to come to Boston, holding out all the inducements which this field offered for the salvation of souls. After informing his ordinary, the Bishop of Mans, of his intention of crossing the Atlantic, he received an affectionate letter from the aged prelate, who was also an exile, praising his zeal yet urging him to wait for better days. But his determination was fixed, and receiving permission, he took passage in a vessel bound for Boston, arriving here on the 3d of October, 1796.

Rev. J. L. de Cheverus was everyway a suitable associate

for Dr. Matignon. Born on the 28th of January, 1768, he was only about 28 years of age, but of ripe judgment and full of zeal for missionary work. He was ordained priest in December, 1790, at the last public ordination in Paris before the revolution. He was parish priest of his native parish when the bloody persecution of the clergy began, and having refused to take the impious oath proposed by the revolutionists, he was forced to flee. After a short confinement in prison, he repaired to Paris, where he lay concealed during the terrible massacre of the clergy. He left Paris disguised in a military dress, and having procured a passport bearing the name of his brother, he escaped to England.

With such an experience as this, Father de Cheverus was ready for any hardships in the New World. Immediately upon his arrival in Boston, he wrote to Bishop Carroll, and was appointed to the Indian Mission of Maine. He accepted it cheerfully. "Send me where you think I am most needed," he wrote, "without making yourself anxious about the means of supporting me. I am willing to work with my hands, if need be, and I believe I have strength enough for it." He reached Point Pleasant, Passamaquoddy Bay, on the 30th of July, 1797, and immediately took up his abode in a house erected for him. "My house," he wrote, "is about ten feet square and eight feet high, and the church, as large again, but not a great deal higher. In both no other material than bark, and a few logs of wood and sticks set up crossways to support the bark; no windows, of course — the only opening is a door. The only piece of furniture is a large table made of two rough boards. The altar-piece is made of two pieces of broadcloth,— the one of scarlet, and the other of dark blue."

Father Cheverus continued his missionary labors in Maine for about two years, visiting the Indian settlements on the Kennebec, Penobscot and Passamaquoddy Bay, till he was relieved by Rev. James Romagne, a townsman of his own, who was sent here by Bishop Carroll for that special work. This zealous clergyman was joyfully welcomed by both Fathers Matignon and Cheverus, and immediately proceeded to his apostolic mission. He took up the work of his predecessor, and, as Father Fitton says, "he restored piety and religion, corrected abuses, encouraged industry, and trained all to God during the eighteen years he remained." Owing to failing health he returned to France in 1818, where he performed spiritual duties till his death in 1836.

With Dr. Matignon, Father Cheverus was now enabled to devote his whole time to the Boston mission, which included the various towns in Massachusetts, and the rapid progress of the Church under their ministrations, shows how successfully they worked. "Their tasks, their pursuits, their dispositions, were kindred, and they became inseparable," writes Father Fitton, "and their many virtues and social qualities were the admiration even of their adversaries." Another writer says:—"The Bostonians were charmed. In the persons of her ministers, Catholicity became respected and honored, where before it had only been a reproach. Never did virtue and learning gain a more decided victory over prejudice and intolerance." The parochial residence was a house on School street, two doors from the church. The preaching of these two learned priests attracted many Protestants as well as Catholics to the little church on School street, and the regular congregation steadily increased. It soon became evident that a larger place of worship was needed, and the lease of the little building having nearly expired, the members determined to purchase a lot and build a suitable church. With this end in view, they assembled at their place of worship on Sunday, March 31, 1799, and appointed a committee to consider the matter and report on the next Sunday. This committee was composed as follows:—The Spanish Consul Don Juan Stoughton, John Magner, Patrick Campbell, Michael Burns, Owen Callahan, John Duggan, and Edmund Connor.

On the following Sunday, April 7, a report was submitted, declaring the need of a new church, and it was unanimously resolved to purchase a lot and start a subscription, Rev. Drs. Matignon and Cheverus being appointed Treasurers. Subscription books were opened the same day, and two hundred and twelve persons had subscribed $3,202; one person gave $333; two gave $250 each, and eight $100 each. The Protestant community generously contributed, and at the head of these donors was the name of the venerable John Adams, President of the United States. Dr. Matignon solicited aid from Catholic friends at the South, and the total amount raised before the church was completed was $16,153.52, as follows:—From members of congregation $10,771.69; other Catholics, $1,948.83; Protestants, $3,433.

The following list of Catholic subscribers in the diocese of Boston, to the Franklin street Church, is worthy of a place in this connection:—

Cavanagh & Cottrell, of Damariscotta, Me.
John Magner.
Patrick Campbell.
Michael Burns.
Edmund Connor.
Owen Callahan.
John Downy.
Mrs. Lobb.
Mrs. Doyle.
James Watt.
Joseph Costello.
John Ward.
John Moriarty.
Stephen Roberts.
Rev. C. H. M.
Wm. Barry.
Michael Connolly.
Lawrence Grant.
Mrs. Torpey.
James Cavanagh.
Abraham S. Hony.
Michael Hefferman.
Daniel English.

James Foley.
Eleanor Noldon.
Stephen Feeney.
Patrick Walsh (at Shays.)
William Flint.
Stephen Shells.
Mrs. Cummins.
Francis Maguire.
James Maguire.
John Bull.
John Hurley.
Peter Fitzpatrick.
Walter Landregan.
Michael Neoff.
AnnahWilliam.
Richard Murphy.
John Dowlen.
Black Joseph Jean Louis.
Felix Morgan.
The Viscount of Grenier.
John Driscat.
David Fitzgerald and John his little boy.
William Daly.

Richard Shays.
John Pew said Quinn.
James Shays.
James Forrester.
Martin Freeman.
Andrew Cummins.
Patrick Wall.
John Whelan.
Peter Lenemany.
Manon Flamason.
James Cox (South End,
Francaise.
Noel Simon.
Jean Tanguey.
Daniel Callahan.
Patrick Welch (of Kilk, at T. Murphy's).
Peter Collins.
Joseph Louis.
Maurice Torpey.
Michael White.

Isaac Doe.	Augustine Gallet.	Simon Hamirault.
Daniel Manning.	Abraham Fitton.	Elizabeth Stevens.
Thomas Kilmartin.	Robert Guery.	Catharine Downing
Patrick Griffith.	Michael Gonagh.	Thomas Murphy.
Michael Griffith.	John Danie.	Thomas Coghran.
Michael Kilby.	Chas. Peverslly.	Black Jiny.
James Shay.	John Cox.	James Cox.
Sally Chapman.	John de Crux.	

The list of Protestant subscribers includes about one hundred and forty, and takes in nearly all the leading families at that time. Besides President Adams, we find the names of Perkins, Higginson, Mason, Lyman, Parkman, Parker, Coolidge, Bussey, Derby, Sears, Preble, Prince, Greene, Walter, Cox, Blake, J. Q. Adams, Dexter, Heard, Fales, Brooks, J. Quincy, Dunlap, Stackpole, Amory, S. Tuckerman, Loring, Andrew, Brigham, H. G. Otis, Lowell, S. Breck, Elliot, Shaw, Cobb, Warren, Jackson, Weld, Sturgis, Russell, Sheaf, Hunnewell, Wiswall, Bradley, Winslow, Peabody, Crowningshield, West, Gray, Pierce, Prescott, and others.

At another meeting held October 28, 1799, a report was presented, recommending the purchase of a site at the end of Franklin place, afterwards Franklin street, belonging to the Boston Theatre Corporation, who had, five years before, completed the new theatre on Federal street. The corporation stated that they preferred to sell the property at a lower rate for a Catholic church, than for a tavern or other public house. The report was accepted, the land bought for $2,500, and deeded to Bishop Carroll and Dr. Matignon, trustees. The same lot was sold in 1860 for $115,000. Ground was broken on St. Patrick's Day, March 17, 1800, and the work of building progressed slowly for three years, the good priests not being desirous of pushing the work faster than the money to pay for it was received.

James Bulfinch, Esq., generously furnished the plan of the church and superintended the work gratis, for which he received the thanks of the congregation and an elegant silver urn, valued at $165. The church measured eighty feet in length and sixty in width, and was considered a noble structure for that time. It was the largest and principal Catholic church in New England for many years afterwards. The basement was built of stone and the main structure of brick. The entire cost of the building was twenty thousand dollars. Among the items of expense entered by Dr. Matignon is one which shows the custom of the times. Under date of August 8, 1802, appears the sum of $2.40 for "rum and gin to the people who helped the landing of the timber."

How anxiously the few Catholics of Boston nearly one hundred years ago must have watched the progress of the future Cathedral, and how great must have been their joy when they saw the church completed and ready for divine service. The day fixed for the dedication was the 29th of September, 1803, a day of marked significance for the Catholics in New England. Everything was done in due form. At a little before 10 o'clock, a procession issued from the house of the Spanish consul Don Juan Stoughton, on Franklin place, nearly opposite the new church. Following the cross-bearer were Bishop Carroll, Dr. Matignon, Rev. John L. Cheverus and two other clergymen, with a few altar boys. At the church the ceremony of dedication was performed with great solemnity by the Bishop and his assistant priests, under the name of the "Church of the Holy Cross." After the dedication, Pontifical High Mass was celebrated by the Right Rev. Dr. Carroll, and a sermon preached by Father Cheverus. The collection amounted to $286. The building was crowded to its utmost capacity. About a dozen singers, male and female, formed the choir, and sang the Mass in Gregorian chant, known as the "Missa Regia," Mr. Massé, a Frenchman, presided at the organ; three of his sons formed the bulk of the choir afterwards in Bishop Cheverus' day. Miss Elizabeth Adams, afterwards Mrs. Cox, who visited the first fair for the present Cathedral in 1871, in her 89th year, was one of the singers at the dedication of the Franklin street church. The music, being the first of the kind ever heard in Boston, was highly praised.

The grand altar piece representing the Crucifixion, which became so familiar to succeeding congregations, was painted by Mr. Lawrence Sargent of Boston, for which he received $200. It was worth a much larger sum, but at the suggestion of members of the congregation, he presented the balance to the church.

The bell, which for half a century rang out its solemn and joyous notes from the tower of the Cathedral, was a present from Gen. Elias Hasket Derby, grandfather of Dr. Hasket Derby, the celebrated occulist, who for several years past has given his services to the Carney Hospital. Dr. Derby, who is a convert, and now a member of the Cathedral congregation, takes great pride in the spirit shown by his grandfather. It seems that there is a little romance attached to this affair. Gen. Derby, when a young man, visited his future wife at her father's residence, on Franklin street. Sitting with her one Sunday at the window, after the new church was opened, he noticed the people going to worship. But the belfry of the new church was silent, and he learned that it was because the congregation was too poor to buy a bell. As he was a prosperous merchant with his father, and had ships trading with Europe, he conceived the idea of sending abroad for a bell and presenting it to the church. It is supposed that the young lady encouraged him in his generous proposition, for it was not long before the bell was brought from Europe in one of his own vessels and presented to the church. Dr. Matignon and Bishop Cheverus afterwards became quite intimate with the family, and were visitors at his residence. The bell was obtained in Italy or Spain, but nobody knows from whom. It bears an inscription which shows that a certain Leopold de Nicolini, and his wife, Theresa, caused the bell to be made in 1798, in honor of God and our Lady of the Rosary. After having done good service in the Cathedral tower, it now welcomes the funeral processions to Holyhood

Cemetery. "Many a one," says Father Healy, "to whom its sound was familiar in youth has been laid to rest, while the old bell repeated its unvarying sound of sorrow, and the cross which they loved to see in Franklin place, shines brightly over their graves. Both were given for safe keeping to Holyhood Cemetery until a new Cathedral should claim them."

The following record of the baptisms, marriages, and deaths, during the first ten years of the Catholic church in Boston will be interesting:—

Years.	Baptisms.	Marriages.	Deaths.
1790	30	1	4
1791	23	3	4
1792	15	4	2
1793	28	12	11
1794	42	5	18
1795	40	5	9
1796	47	11	6
1797	60	11	10
1798	59	26	34
1799	77	18	8

In their new church, Dr. Matignon and his Rev. colleague worked with greater zeal than ever and their congregation steadily increased. They opened a day school for boys in the tower of the church, in a room immediately under the bell deck. This was the first Catholic school in Boston, where, Father Fitton tells us, he "was initiated in the elements of a spelling book." Five years later, in 1808, Boston was made an Episcopal See by Pope Pius VII., but, in consequence of the troubles in Europe at that period, the bulls did not reach America until 1810, when it was learned that His Holiness had appointed Rev. JOHN L. DE CHEVERUS FIRST BISHOP OF BOSTON. This appointment had been effected at the solicitation of Rev. Dr. Matignon, with the concurrence and approbation of Rt. Rev. Dr. Carroll. Shortly after the arrival of the credentials from Rome, Dr. de Cheverus was consecrated Bishop by the Most Rev. Dr. Carroll, in the Church of St. Peter, Baltimore, on the feast of All Saints, November 1, 1810.

Bishop Cheverus soon returned to Boston, and continued to occupy his humble dwelling in the rear of the church with his esteemed friend Dr. Matignon, sharing in the minutest duties of the ministry. His first care was to visit his new diocese which comprised all New England, and during his first visitation he confirmed three hundred and forty-eight persons. The good Bishop continued to visit his scattered flock year after year, and had the great satisfaction of seeing new churches and congregations springing up in various parts of his diocese. Among the first priests ordained by Bishop Cheverus for the Boston diocese, were Rev. Denis Ryan and Rev. Patrick Byrne.

Dr. Matignon, after twenty-six years of constant ministerial labors, as pastor of the Holy Cross in Boston, was called to his reward. He died on the 19th of September, 1818, deeply regretted by his loving congregation and the whole diocese. He was "a faithful servant of God, an exemplary pastor, a sincere friend, and a true pattern of a good christian." His remains were borne with due ceremony from the Cathedral to the Granary Burying Ground on Tremont street, and deposited in the tomb of Mr. John Magner, but were subsequently transferred to the new cemetery in South Boston, where they now lie in a vault near the altar of the church. In testimony of the respect in which the faithful priest was held, a large concourse of citizens of all denominations followed the body, first to its temporary tomb, and afterwards to its last resting-place in South Boston.

The following stands on the record of his interment, in the handwriting of Bishop de Cheverus:—

"Sept. 21st * * * Francis Anthony Matignon. D. D., and for twenty-six years Pastor of this congregation — Holy Cross. On Saturday the 19th he died as he lived — a saint. * * * Æt. 65."

The death of Dr. Matignon was a great loss to Boston and the diocese. Bishop Cheverus felt it most severely, and to him it was irreparable. Owing to the small number of priests, the good Bishop was called upon to perform incessant missionary duties, travelling unaccompanied from town to town by the poor conveyances of those days, and it soon became evident that his strength could not stand the strain. His friends in France, hearing of his condition, became anxious about him, and induced Louis XVIII. to nominate him to the bishopric of Montauban, in an ordinance dated January 15, 1823. He at first was disposed to decline the appointment, as he did not want to leave his people in Boston, but physicians declared that he could not endure another winter in this climate. He finally yielded to what he accepted as the will of Providence, and prepared to leave for France.

Before his departure Bishop Cheverus formally transferred his church property and episcopal residence to the diocese. The Ursuline Convent, which he had established a few years before, adjoining the church, with the funds raised by Father Thayer, was included in the transfer. His library which contained many valuable works was left for the benefit of his successors. The remainder of his possessions was distributed "among his ecclesiastics, his friends and the poor," says Father Fitton, "and as he had come to Boston a poor man, he chose to depart poor, with no other wealth than the same trunk, which twenty-seven years before, he had brought with him." On the day of his departure from Boston he was escorted from his residence by a large concourse of citizens, and three hundred vehicles accompanied him many miles on the road to New York.

On the first of October, 1823, the good Bishop embarked at New York for France, and on his arrival there he repaired to his diocese. After a few years he was translated to the Archiepiscopal See of Bordeaux, and subsequently, in recognition of his great services and many virtues, he was raised to the dignity of a Prince of the Church, as Cardinal Archbishop of Bordeaux. He died on 19th of July, 1836. His name is held in deep veneration by the people of France and America.

The following account of the opening of the first Catholic School for young ladies in Boston, under the direction of the

Ursuline Nuns, is taken from Rev. Arthur T. Connolly's historical sketch in the *Pilot* of March 14, 1891 :—

"While the Protestant community was still agitated over the last inroad that Catholicity had made in its ranks, two young ladies arrived in Boston from the city of Limerick, Ire. They were sisters, and the daughters of Mr. James Ryan, a respectable gentleman of Limerick, with whom the Rev. John Thayer had taken up his abode on his arrival in Ireland.

"Mary and Catherine Ryan had been educated in the Ursuline Convent at Thurles, and when Father Thayer had spoken about his desire of establishing an institution for the education of Catholic young ladies at Boston, they entered warmly into his plans and offered to go to America and begin the work.

"When Father Thayer wrote to Bishop Cheverus and made known their desire, the good Bishop immediately accepted their offer, and after making arrangements with the Ursuline Sisters of Three Rivers, Canada, with regard to their novitiate n that community, invited them to come to America without delay.

"The death of Father Thayer, on February 5, 1815, delayed their departure, however, for some time; but true to their vocation, they set sail from Limerick, on May 4, 1817, and not long afterwards presented themselves before Bishop Cheverus. Rejoicing at the thought that he might now undertake the accomplishment of a long-cherished design, he sent them, under the care of Dr. Matignon, to the Ursuline Convent at Three Rivers.

"By a will made by Father Thayer previous to his death, he bequeathed quite a sum of money to Dr. Matignon, to be held in trust by him until such time as an academy might be built or purchased.

"With this fund Bishop Cheverus now secured the house and land next to the Church of the Holy Cross on Franklin place, and there the Misses Ryan, after their solemn profession in the Ursuline Convent at Three Rivers, opened the first Catholic school for young ladies in Boston."

PART IV.

ADMINISTRATION OF BISHOP FENWICK — 1823 TO 1846.

The affairs of the Boston diocese were administered for about two years by the Very Rev. William Taylor, who was made Vicar General by Bishop Cheverus. In 1825, His Holiness, Pope Leo XII., was pleased to fill the vacancy in the Boston See by the appointment of REVEREND BENEDICT JOSEPH FENWICK, a distinguished member of the Society of Jesus. He was born on the 3d of September, 1782, at his father's plantation on Beaver Dam Manor, in St. Mary's County, Maryland, and was a descendant of one of the two hundred families that originally came over from England, under the charter of Lord Baltimore. He was ordained at Georgetown on the 11th of June, 1808, and was sent to New York, where he continued until the Spring of 1817, when he was recalled by his Superior to assume the Presidency of Georgetown College. In the Autumn of 1818, he was sent to Charleston, S. C., to take charge of a troublesome congregation there, and after restoring order he was succeeded by Bishop England and returned to Georgetown. Father Fenwick was performing the duties of President of the College for the second time, when he was called to the vacant See of Boston. Dr. Fenwick was consecrated Bishop in St. Mary's Cathedral, Baltimore, by the Most Rev. Archbishop Marechal, assisted by the Rt. Rev. Dr. England, Bishop of Charleston, and Rt. Rev. Henry Conwell, Bishop of Philadelphia, on the festival of All Saints, November 1, 1825.

Bishop Fenwick started for his diocese as soon as possible, and reached Boston on the third of December. On the following Sunday, he entered the Cathedral of the Holy Cross and was there formally received by Very Rev. William Taylor, who, after his address of welcome, gave the new Bishop an account of the state of the diocese. In concluding his discourse, Father Taylor tendered his resignation and announced his intention of leaving America and returning to Europe. He died in Paris, August, 1828.

Bishop Fenwick was accompanied to Boston by Bishop England and Rev. Virgil H. Barber, S. J. The latter gentleman had been a Protestant minister in New Hampshire, but, through the grace of God, was led to the faith and was received into the church by Dr. Fenwick, in New York. His wife and children also became Catholics and all entered the religious state. Pontifical Mass was celebrated by Bishop Fenwick on the first Sunday, and the sermon was preached by Dr. England, whose eloquence and learning made a deep impression on the vast concourse of people that filled every available space in the Cathedral.

When Bishop Fenwick assumed charge in Boston, the diocese still embraced all New England. His field was wide but his laborers few. He had only one clergyman at his disposal in Boston, Rev. Patrick Byrne; one a hundred miles distant in Maine, Rev. Denis Ryan; and one at Claremont, N. H., Rev. V. H. Barber. The only church in Boston besides the Cathedral was St. Augustine's, in South Boston.

The Bishop's attention was first given to his own immediate congregation, which needed larger accommodations. He immediately had a plan drawn up for the enlargement of the Cathedral, adding a new building 72 feet in width and nearly 40 feet in length, which, with the old church, made one entire edifice of 120 feet in length, including the sacristies, and 72 feet in its widest part. This arrangement afforded school rooms in the basement, and made the Cathedral substantially as known to us in later years. The congregation generously aided the Bishop, and in 1828 he had the satisfaction of seeing the building completed.

While this work was going on the zealous Bishop was preparing several young men for the service of the Church, and during the Ember Days of December, 1827, he promoted two to the holy office of priesthood, Rev. James Fitton and Rev. William Wiley. Father Fitton's parents were members of the first congregation of one hundred who assembled in the small rented building on School street. How long and successfully he labored in the diocese under Bishop Fenwick, Bishop Fitzpatrick and Archbishop Williams, it is unnecessary to record in detail. In East Boston, where he was best known in our time, his memory will be revered by succeeding generations. Father Wiley also served faithfully in East Boston. It was a few months before the ordination of Fathers Fitton and Wiley that our present Archbishop entered the school attached to the Cathedral at the age of five years, under the tutorage of Mr. Fitton.

Before beginning the enlargement of the Cathedral, Bishop Fenwick removed the community of Ursuline Nuns from their cramped up quarters to a new building on the beautiful site in Charlestown, known since as Mt. Benedict. There the good Sisters remained with a flourishing school for young ladies, until they were driven from it, in 1834, by an infuriated mob of bigots, who burned the building and barely allowed the inmates to escape with their lives. This act of gross injustice remains to be compensated for by the state.

Notwithstanding the sad disappointment which the destruction of the convent school caused the good Bishop, he continued to labor energetically for his diocese, and he had the pleasure of seeing new churches, with numerous priests, established all around him. St. Mary's church in Charlestown was started in 1828. St. Mary's, Pond street, afterwards Endicott street, was dedicated in 1836, and St. Patrick's, Northampton street, was completed in 1836. After a few years, other churches were opened in Boston, including St. John's, Moon street; SS. Peter's and Paul's, South Boston; and the German Church, Suffolk street. Before his death, Bishop Fenwick had in Boston eight churches, six of which were built during his administration.

In 1844, Massachusetts alone had 21 priests, 22 churches, and 10 stations, with a Catholic population of 53,000.

St. Vincent's Orphan Asylum was started in Boston, under the patronage of Bishop Fenwick, in 1832, by Sister Ann Alexis, Sister Blandina and Sister Loyola. They at first opened a free school for girls in Hamilton street. Nine years afterwards a building was purchased for them on the corner of High and Pearl streets, where the asylum was established. In 1845, a commodious house on Purchase street was secured for their use, and there they remained till their present large building on Camden street was ready for occupancy.

Holy Cross College at Worcester, was founded by Bishop Fenwick in 1842, and given by him to the Jesuits Fathers in 1843.

After twenty-one years of continuous labor in the care of souls as Bishop of Boston, the Rt. Rev. Benedict J. Fenwick went to his reward. He died on the 11th of August, 1846. His body was taken to Worcester, and buried in the grounds of the College. Dr. Brownson, in an article on the death of the Bishop, wrote:—"His monument is in the grateful recollections of his people, whom he fed with the bread of life, and governed with equal affection and wisdom for over twenty years. Everywhere in his diocese we may read the proofs of his paternal solicitude, his wisdom and energy, his devotion to the people of his charge, and of his having lived and labored with no thought but for the greater glory of God, and the advancement of the Church. He found his diocese with only three small churches and one priest; he left it with nearly fifty churches and as many priests. He relieved the poor, paid especial attention to the education and training of the young, and finally crowned his well-spent life with the erection of that noble monument to his love of learning and his zeal for his people, the College of the Holy Cross at Worcester, where the grateful student long shall kneel at his tomb."

PART V.

ADMINISTRATION OF BISHOP FITZPATRICK — 1846 TO 1866.

The RIGHT REV. JOHN BERNARD FITZPATRICK was the third Bishop of Boston. He was consecrated Coadjutor to Bishop Fenwick in 1844, and administered under the authority of his Superior until the latter's death in 1846. Bishop Fitzpatrick was born in Boston November 1, 1812. His parents were natives of Tullamore, Kings County, Ireland, and emigrated to this country in 1805. They were steadfast adherents to the ancient faith, and the father was one of the leading Catholics under Dr. Matignon and Bishop Cheverus, both of whom honored his house on the evening of his son's baptism.

John Bernard received his early education at the public schools He passed through the primary and grammar, in the Adams and Boylston, and bore off two Franklin medals, of which he felt justly proud. He excelled in every branch of study, more especially in mathematics, declamation and rhetoric. In 1826, when 14 years of age, he entered the Boston Latin School, then under the charge of Master Leverett and Submaster Parker, and remained there three years, passing successful examinations in Greek and Latin, with other higher studies, carrying off two more medals. His assiduity won the respect and admiration of his masters, and his general conduct, the esteem and love of his school-fellows. During these years he was a constant attendant at church and catechism, and never was so happy as when permitted to serve the priest at the altar.

After graduating from the Latin School at 17 years of age, he was sent to the Montreal Seminary, it being the design of his parents and his Bishop, as well as his own inclination, that he should be educated for the priesthood. He remained in

Montreal eight years, and passed through Boston, on his way to Paris, where he entered the grand Seminary of St. Sulpice in 1837. He completed there his course of theological studies with distinction, and was ordained priest on the eve of Trinity Sunday, December, 1840.

Father Fitzpatrick spent nearly a year abroad, and then returned to his native city to begin his ministerial work. After a year of pastoral duties at the Cathedral, and as associate pastor at St. Mary's, North End, he was appointed pastor of East Cambridge, where he built the church of St. John, from which he was called to be Coadjutor to Bishop Fenwick.

When Bishop Fitzpatrick took charge of the See of Boston his diocese comprised Massachusetts, Maine, New Hampshire, and Vermont; Rhode Island and Connecticut having been cut off and erected into the See of Hartford in 1844, under the government of Rt. Rev. William Tyler. Being full of vigor and zeal, Bishop Fitzpatrick carried the burden of administering the diocese alone for ten years, not having a Secretary till 1855, when Rev. James A. Healy, (now Bishop of Portland,) was selected for that office. Bishop Healy was the first and only secretary of Bishop Fitzpatrick, and he continued the trusted assistant of his superior until the latter's eyes were closed in death. No Vicar General was assigned until 1857, when our present Archbishop was appointed. In these early years the good Bishop overtaxed his strength, and his painful illness later was probably the result of this overwork.

The fruits of the Bishop's labors were soon seen on every hand. New religious orders and communities were introduced. Religious and charitable societies were organized. New schools and academies were opened. The magnificent Orphan Asylum was completed. Boston College and the Church of the Immaculate Conception, in charge of the Jesuit Fathers, were built. And new churches and institutions multiplied in all parts of his diocese. It has been truly remarked, that during Bishop Fitzpatrick's administration, the tone of public opinion towards

Catholicity had experienced a complete change, and that Protestant Boston had become one of the strongest Catholic cities in the Union.

The old Cathedral building on Franklin street became too small and inconvenient for the wants of the congregation, and as its timbers showed signs of decay, it had to be abandoned. The street improvements and great demand for store property in that neighborhood made the site of the church quite valuable, and it was sold to Mr. Isaac Rich, who replaced the sanctified building by a business structure, which, before being defaced by the great fire in 1872, bore the inscription "Cathedral Building."

On the 16th of September, 1860, almost half a century after its dedication, the last Divine Services were performed in the dear old Franklin street Cathedral of the Holy Cross. Bishop Fitzpatrick celebrated Pontifical High Mass, assisted by the present Archbishop; Father Fitton, who had been baptized, confirmed and ordained there; and Rev. Michael Moran, present pastor of St. Stephen's. "The Bishop bore up bravely," states Rt. Rev. Jas. A. Healy, in a lecture delivered a few years afterwards, "but at times he could not conceal the almost agony of his heart. The intensity of his feelings, though completely masked from the congregation, would not allow him to speak to them on the final day."

Bishop Fitzpatrick's letter, which was read instead of a sermon, concluded as follows:—

"And now, beloved brethren, the Cathedral of the Holy Cross, under its present form, must needs be discontinued; another, under the same title, the same holy banner, must take its place, and this is our work. To-day, for the last time, we offer on this altar the Holy Sacrifice of the Mass. Let us, in most fervent union with the Divine Victim, who there offers Himself for us, return thanks to God for the numberless and precious blessings which, through this venerable temple have come down upon our country, and upon ourselves. Let us pour out our supplications of charity for the souls of our prelates, our pastors, our confessors, our brethren who have worshipped here, before us or with us. Let us implore the bestowal of divine grace upon all and every one of us, that no one may depart from this Altar to-day without the resolution of laboring for the beauty of God's house, and of co-operating generously and perseveringly for the erection of a new Cathedral of the Holy Cross, which may promote for ages to come the glory of God and the salvation of souls,

OLD CATHEDRAL, FRANKLIN STREET.

set before the world the splendor and majesty of Catholic worship, and be to us, and to all who may come after us, a just reason of pious exultation and of holy pride."

Bishop Healy thus eloquently describes the closing service:— "But who can forget the last solemn Vespers and Benediction of the Blessed Sacrament, on the same day? Never did the Cathedral witness a more imposing or touching ceremony. The silent majesty of the Sanctuary, the three altars beautifully illuminated, the Bishop's throne, the clergy present, all come back in vivid remembrance. The solemn silence of the Benediction, broken only by the sound of the little bell; the kneeling clergy and people, the lights, the flowers, the altars, and in the midst and over all, the majestic form of the venerable and beloved Bishop, holding for the last time in his life the Blessed Lord to bless the people of the Holy Cross! When all was over and the clergy departed, few left the church. The mass of the people lingered in their seats or sauntered through the aisles, or crowded around the Sanctuary, observant of all, anxious even for a flower that had been upon the Altar. The gay array of lights was allowed to shine for a long, long time, but at length the final moment came, the last light was extinguished, the last worshipper departed, and the doors of the Cathedral were closed, never to be re-opened except to the destroyer. Such, my friends, was the closing of the old Cathedral of the Holy Cross."

The failing health of Bishop Fitzpatrick and the financial troubles incident to the early days of the Southern Rebellion, delayed the commencement of the new Cathedral, for which land at the South End had been purchased in 1859. The Melodeon on Washington street was hired for services on Sundays, under the rectorship of Rev. James A. Healy, but only a remnant of the old congregation was kept together, the people having scattered to various parts of the city and into other parishes. A large hall on Beach street accommodated the children of the Sunday School. The episcopal residence was removed to No. 6 South street.

In the autumn of 1862, the church on the corner of Washington and Castle streets was purchased from the Unitarians, and the Cathedral parish was transferred from the centre of the city to the South End. The first services in this Pro-Cathedral were held on the 10th of December, 1862, and the episcopal residence was removed to the house on the corner of the lot on Washington street, bought for the new Cathedral. Bishop Fitzpatrick's health continued to fail, and he went abroad for a time in hopes of a restoration. But he returned very little improved, and after long and patient suffering, "his pure spirit returned to God who gave it. He died as he had lived, like a Bishop." A few weeks before his death, the venerated Bishop had the satisfaction of knowing that his beloved flock would be well cared for by his able Coadjutor, Dr. Williams. Bishop Fitzpatrick died on the 13th of February, 1866. His remains are deposited in the crypt under the sanctuary of the new Cathedral.

CLERGYMEN ATTACHED TO THE CHURCH IN SCHOOL STREET.

Rev. C. de la Poterie,	Rev. John Cheverus,
L. S. Rousselet,	(afterwards Bishop.)
John Thayer,	J. S. Tisserand,
F. A. Matignon.	

CLERGYMEN ATTACHED TO THE CATHEDRAL IN FRANKLIN PLACE.

Under Bishop Cheverus.

Rev. F. A. Matignon,	Rev. P. Larrissy, O. S. A.
J. S. Tisserand,	Paul McQuade,
Matthew O'Brien,	Patrick Byrne,
Denis Ryan,	William Taylor,
J. Romagne,	(was V. G.)

Under Bishop Fenwick.

Rev. Michael Healy, (was V. G.)	Rev. Wm. Fennelly,
James Fitton,	Edward Walsh, (was V. G.)
Wm. Wiley,	Patrick McNamee,
Patrick Smith,	Michael Gaibens,
Wm. Tyler,	Francis Rolof,
(was V. G., and	James O'Reilly,
afterwards Bishop	James Strain,
of Hartford.)	Thos. J. O'Flaherty,
R. D. Woodley,	A. Williamson,
(afterwards S. J.)	Richard B. Hardy,
Patrick O'Beirne,	James Maguire,
James Smith,	J. B. Fitzpatrick,
P. McDermott,	(afterwards Bishop
Thomas Lynch,	of Boston.)

Rev. Michael Lynch,
    John Brady,
    John D. Brady,
    James Conway,
    John Mahony,
    Peter Connolly,
    Chas. Ffrench, O. S. D.
    James Edward Lee,
    John Corry,
    John J. Curtin,
    James Drummond,
    B. O'Cavanagh,
    Patrick Flood.

Rev. N. J. O'Brien,
    Geo. F. Haskins.
    P. F. Lyndon,
    (was V. G. of Boston.)
    Peter Crudden,
    John J. Williams,
    (was V. G., and is now Archbishop of Boston.
    Ambrose Manahan,
    Charles E. Brasseur de Bourbourg.

Under Bishop Fitzpatrick.

Rev. John J. Doherty,
    John O'Donnell,
    (was V. G. of Portland.)
    M. P. Galligher,
    Samuel A. Mullcdy,
    P. O. Allaire,
    Thos. H. Shahan,
    Geo. T. Riordan,
    J. M. Finotti,
    Hilary Tucker,
    A. M. Baret,

Rev. Jas. A. Healy,
    (now Bishop of Portland.)
    P. J. Rogers,
    John T. Roddan,
    Jos. P. Tallon,
    Michael Moran,
    Chas. Lynch,
    J. Lionnet,
    L. S. McMahon,
    (now Bishop of Hartford.)
    Wm. Byrne, (now V. G.)

PART VI.

ADMINISTRATION OF ARCHBISHOP WILLIAMS.

The clergy and laity were unaminous in the opinion that no ecclesiastic in the diocese was better qualified to govern the See of Boston than the RT. REV. JOHN J. WILLIAMS. The success of his high mission after twenty-five years of devoted service is a conclusive proof of the wisdom that inspired his selection, and the numerous demonstrations of respect and loyalty paid him on the anniversary of his consecration, show how highly he is appreciated by all classes in the community. Among all the venerated prelates of the Catholic Hierarchy in the United States, no one is more sincerely loved by the clergy and laity than the present occupant of the Archiepiscopal See of Boston.

Archbishop Williams was born in Boston, April 27, 1822. His parents were Irish Catholics, who landed here in 1818, and were among the first Catholic emigrants who came direct from Ireland to Boston. The vessel in which they were passengers was bound to Halifax, N. S., but for some cause or other arrived first at the port of Boston. The father of our Archbishop was a native of the County of Tipperary, and his mother was born in Queen's County. The parents first settled at the North End of the city, and when their second child John Joseph was born, they were living in a house which backed on the old canal, near the present location of the New England House on Blackstone street. The family subsequently removed to a house on Broad street, which was the home of the future Archbishop during his early boyhood. The first school he attended while a mere child, was a public primary on Hamilton street, in charge of a Mrs. Newmarch, and for about a year he was a regular public school scholar.

This was the only public school in which he received any instruction.

At the age of five years he was sent to the school conducted by Bishop Fenwick, under the sanctuary of the Franklin street Cathedral. Here he was placed in a class in charge of Rev. James Fitton, who was then with other students, preparing for the priesthood, and who was ordained the same year. Father Fitton, the zealous missionary and faithful pastor of East Boston for many years, lived to see his pupil made Archbishop of Boston. Young Williams remained a diligent scholar at this first parochial school for about six years, when, under the direction of Bishop Fenwick, in 1833, the youthful student was sent to the Seminary of St. Sulpice, in Montreal. In the same class with Master Williams, just before he left Boston, was Mr. Bernard Foley, now an active merchant of Boston, and the only known living member of the class besides the Archbishop.

At the Montreal Seminary, young Williams pursued his classical studies until 1841, when he graduated at the age of nineteen, a candidate for the priesthood. In order to complete his theological course, he went to Paris, and there entered the Grand Seminary of St. Sulpice, the great seat of learning from which Father Fitzpatrick had graduated only a year before. After successfully passing his four years' course, he was, in 1845, ordained priest by Mgr. Affre, Archbishop of Paris.

Father Williams returned to his native city of Boston in October, 1845, and became an assistant priest at the Cathedral under his beloved Bishop Fenwick, who died about a year afterwards. Under Bishop Fitzpatrick he continued at the Cathedral for about ten years, giving special attention to the Sunday School for eight years, and performing the duties of rector the two last years. A large number of men and women in Boston to-day remember with pleasure the instructions given them by Father Williams, while they were members of his Sunday School. In 1857, he was assigned to the pastorate of St. James Church, Albany street, and two years afterwards was appointed Vicar General by Bishop Fitzpatrick. Father Williams labored successfully for nine years in St. James, which under his charge became one of the most important parishes in Boston.

As Vicar General, owing to the failing health of Bishop Fitzpatrick, Father Williams was called upon to administer the affairs of the diocese, and on January 9, 1866, he was appointed Coadjutor to the Bishop under the title of Bishop of Tripoli, with right of succession. Before arrangements were completed for his consecration, the Boston See became vacant by the death of Bishop Fitzpatrick, on the 13th of February, 1866, and a month later, Dr. Williams was consecrated Bishop of Boston.

In St. James Church, this grand ceremony of consecration took place, on the 11th of March, 1866, in the presence of a large assemblage of bishops and priests, and of his devoted parishioners. Archbishop McCloskey, of New York, afterwards Cardinal, was the consecrator, assisted by Bishops De Goesbriand of Burlington, Bacon of Portland, McFarland of Hartford, and Loughlin of Brooklyn.

After his consecration, Bishop Williams removed to the episcopal residence, corner of Union Park and Washington streets, on the site which had been previously purchased by Bishop Fitzpatrick for the new Cathedral. The Cathedral congregation was then in possession of the church corner of Castle and Washington streets, under charge of Rev. James A. Healy, who was rector from 1857 until 1866, and who stood faithfully by his flock in its migrations from the old Franklin street Cathedral to the Melodeon and thence to the Castle street church, which was purchased from the Unitarians. Father Healy was transferred to the pastorship of St. James, to fill the place made vacant by the promotion of Bishop Williams, and remained there until he was elevated to the See of Portland in 1875.

Bishop Williams lost no time in carrying out the cherished wish of his predecessor in regard to the building of a new

Cathedral, and with the able assistance of Very Rev. P. F. Lyndon, who was appointed Vicar General and Rector of the Cathedral, steps were taken for its erection. Ground was broken on the 27th of April 1866, and the corner stone was laid on Sunday, September 15, 1867, with magnificent ceremony and in the presence of the largest assemblage ever gathered in Boston to witness a similar event.

Vicar General Lyndon was placed in immediate charge of the erection of the Cathedral, and only those who lived nearby and saw him day after day superintend the work can appreciate how faithfully he attended to his duties. If ever a structure was well started from its very foundations, it was the present new Cathedral, under Bishop Williams and his energetic Vicar General. Many business men living today will remember how methodical Father Lyndon was in his business affairs and how exacting he was in the performance of all contracts. He was just the man to superintend a great building. He lived to see the Cathedral practically completed.

The following is a list of the principal subscribers who responded to a call made by the Bishop at a meeting held in the basement of Castle street church:—

Joseph Iasigi.
Thomas Dwight.
James Collins.
Mrs. Andrew Carney.
Patrick Donahoe.
Patrick Deavir.
Michael Doherty.
Bernard Foley.
Michael Gleeson.
Arthur McAvoy.
Francis McLaughlin.
Theodore Metcalf.
John Miller.
Nicholase Reggio.
Gabrielle de la Motte.

Patrick Harkins.
Peter Higgins.
M. H. Keenan.
Jacob Kohler.
Bernard McKenna.
John M. Phillips.
Maurice Curry.
Gen. Guiney.
William Maflyn.
Dr. J. G. Blake.
Daniel Ellard.
John Ring.
Thomas C. Pazolt.
Michael Leary.
William Moakely.

John Conlan.
John Boman.
William A. Boyle.
Hugh Carey.
John Finnegan.
John Glancy.
William Hyland.
Joseph A. Laforme.
Robert Moore.
James Power.
Francis Supple.
Joseph Walker.
William White.
John Sullivan.
Henry C. McLaughlin.
Michael A. Ring and Sons.
Malachy Clark.
Patrick Dougherty.
Dennis O'Brien.
Samuel Tuckerman.
Daniel Carney.
John Donovan.
William Doran.
James Gleeson.
Daniel Gilfeather.
Frank Gilfeather.
Robert McDevitt.
John W. McDonald.
Daniel McConologue.
Patrick McCarthy.
James Tallon.
Patrick Murtagh.
Chas. F. Donnelly.
Patrick Kelly.
James McCormick.
John Noonan.
John Shea.
Dennis Collins.

John Reardon.
Peter McAleer.
Francis McClinchy.
E. J. Nagle.
John Noonan.
Jeremiah O'Leary.
Aloysius Ochs.
James Scully.
Peter C. Scott.
John F. Brine.
William Brine.
Andrew Callaghan.
Florence Donellan.
Michael Moore.
Dens. McGillicuddy.
M. H. Bradley.
Eugene Geary.
Bernard Corr.
Thomas Gorman.
Col. P. T. Hanley.
Anthony Bentz.
M. C. Dowling.
E. Gerhard.
D. Hutchinson.
John Mullin.
Francis J. Kraft.
John W. Bragden.
James Barrett.
Dr. Peter D. Walsh.
William Doogue.
Daniel Holland.
David Grady.
John Shea.
James Aylward.
Michael Brennan.
John Paine.
W. J. Mellen.
Dr. Patrick Morris.

William Blakely.
Andrew Cassidy.
Capt. H. Cummiskey.
William Denvir.
Philip Dougherty.
Hugh O'Brien.
Richard Downs.
Patrick Farrell.
Thos. A. Farrand.
Thos. J. Gargan.

Dr. Hugh Ferguson.
Charles O'Neil.
R. O'Connor.
Thomas Power.
John Roach.
William Barter.
Daniel Gallivan.
Dr. Ryan.
P. J. Quirk.

The total sum subscribed at the first meeting was about $36,000. One person gave $3,000, one $2,000, twelve $1,000 each, thirteen $500 to $800 each, eighteen $200 to $300 seven $110 to $175, thirty-three $100 each, and others from $20 to $75 each. Numerous other sums were afterwards added.

During the progress of the building, three fairs were held for the purpose of raising funds. The first was in November, 1871, in the new structure when it was roofed in and a temporary flooring laid. The second was in November, 1874, before the pews were put in. The third was held October 27, 1879, in Castle street church, after the Cathedral had been dedicated. The writer had the privilege of assisting at all these successful efforts for the Cathedral, and can testify to the earnestness and enthusiasm with which, not only the Cathedral people, but all the Catholics in Boston worked to aid their beloved prelate in accomplishing one of the grandest objects of his episcopacy.

Early in 1875, Pope Pius IX., of blessed memory, was pleased to raise the diocese of Boston to an archdiocese, and on May 2nd of the same year, Bishop Williams was made an Archbishop, receiving the pallium from the hands of Cardinal McCloskey. The grand ceremony took place in the new Cathedral before it was dedicated. Long before the services began the vast building was filled to overflowing by an orderly concourse of people. The attendance of the Papal

Ablegate, Mgr. Cesar Roncetti, accompanied by his secretary, the late Rev. Dr. Ubaldi, and Count Marofoschi of the Papal Guards, together with several bishops and a large number of priests, made the occasion one to be remembered by every person present.

On the Feast of the Immaculate, December 8, 1875, the new Cathedral of the Holy Cross was dedicated by Archbishop Williams and opened for divine service. This was the occasion of another grand ceremony and an immense congregation, and was only equalled by the great assemblage on Thursday, March 12, 1891, at the Jubilee Mass in honor of the 25th anniversary of the consecration of our beloved Archbishop.

To go away from the Cathedral, and to give even a brief summary of the rapid progress of the Catholicity in the diocese, would take up more space than was intended for this sketch. When Bishop Williams assumed charge of the diocese, his jurisdiction embraced the whole state of Massachusetts. In 1870, a division was made at the Bishop's suggestion, by the erection of the See of Springfield, comprising the western counties of Berkshire, Franklin, Hampshire, Hampden and Worcester, which was placed in charge of Rt. Rev. P. T. O'Reilly, from Worcester. In 1872 another division was made by setting off a portion of southern Massachusetts with Rhode Island, and establishing the See of Providence, of which Rt. Rev. Thomas F. Hendricken was made the first Bishop. The present administrator of the See is Rt. Rev. Matthew Harkins, D. D., who is a native of Boston, and was a priest at the Cathedral.

The present Archdiocese of Boston is still quite large for one administrator. Under its authority are upwards of 350 priests, about 170 churches, and more than 500,000 souls. What a change from one hundred years ago, when the congregation of the little church on School street numbered less than one hundred persons, and was the only Catholic place of worship in New England outside of the Indian missions in Maine!

In the city of Boston alone, the list of charitable and educational institutions established during the episcopacy of our present Archbishop shows a wonderful growth. It is a record that any prelate should be proud of, and speaks volumes for his clear foresight and wise judgment. Every want seems to be provided for, but he has still other projects in view, which, with God's help and the united assistance of his people, will be accomplished in good time.

Under his administration we have the Home for Destitute Children, which cares for about 500 deserted children every year; the St. Mary's Infant Asylum, which protects the abandoned babes; the Working Boys' Home, which offers a home for the industrious lads who are without kindred or frends; the Nuns of the Good Shepherd, who shelter and reform wayward females; the Little Sisters of the Poor, who cheerfully beg and labor for the comfort of helpless old men and women; the Sisters of St. Francis, who, in their two hospitals, nurse the sick and dying; the Carney Hospital, whose Sisters of Charity never refuse to take in a poor patient; the Brothers of House of the Angel Guardian, who are faithfully educating boys whose dispositions require them to be under restraint; St. Joseph's Home, for the care of children and destitute servant girls under charge of the Franciscan Sisters; and the Home for Working Girls, under care of the Gray Nuns from Montreal.

With this list of charitable institutions comes the Society of St. Vincent de Paul, with its 33 Conferences distributed all over the city and suburbs, caring for the poor in each parish without distinction of creed or race, and saving children who have been abandoned by depraved and criminal parents. The first Conference of this noble Society was organized in St. James parish, under the spiritual direction of our Archbishop, and it is through his active interest and support that the Society has its Conferences in so many of the parishes in the diocese.

Among the numerous societies of Catholic laymen in Boston none holds closer relations with the Archbishop than the Catholic Union. It was organized at his suggestion in 1873, and under his Honorary Presidency has had a steady growth. It has a membership of about four hundred, comprising nearly all the prominent Catholics of the city and suburbs, and its influence is felt all over the diocese. His Grace is a constant attendant at its meetings, and takes an active interest in all its proceedings. At the informal gatherings on Wednesday evenings he is the earliest in the parlors, and there he mingles with the members as one of themselves. He joins freely in all the discussions and shows that he keeps well informed on all the live topics of the day. It is there that his real character can be appreciated. No person can be an hour in his company without feeling impressed by his earnest, sympathetic heart, and his clear, judicial mind. All must be convinced that no prelate could be more truly devoted to his flock, his country and his religion than the present Archbishop of Boston.

Among the educational institutions founded during the episcopacy of Archbishop Williams, the most important is St. John's Ecclesiastical Seminary, in Brighton. It was organized under the direction of very Rev. John Hogan, D. D., who came from the celebrated Sulpician Seminary in Paris, on the solicitation of our Archbishop. Abbe Hogan, being called to the Catholic University in Washington, has been succeeded by Very Rev. Chas. B. Rex, S.S., who is assisted by an efficient corps of professors. The Archbishop clearly saw the need of an institution of this kind, where candidates for the priesthood could be educated under his own supervision, and he has made the Seminary the object of his special care. It will prove to be one of the richest fruits of his episcopacy.

Many other institutions of learning have received his attention and patronage. Besides the Boston College, in charge of the Jesuit Fathers, there are the two Academies of Notre Dame, the Academy of the Sacred Heart, with parochial schools at the Cathedral, St. James, St. Mary's, St. Joseph's, St. Patrick's,

Holy Trinity; S.S. Peter and Paul's, South Boston; Gate of Heaven, South Boston; Holy Redeemer, East Boston; Our Lady of the Assumption, East Boston; Sacred Heart, East Boston; and Leo XIII. School, Jamaica Plain. Outside of Boston, in the Archdiocese, there are parochial and convent schools in Amesbury, Arlington, Brockton, Cambridgeport, Cambridge, Canton, Chelsea, Gloucester, Haverhill, Hyde Park, Lawrence, Lowell, Lynn, Malden, Marlboro', Newburyport, Salem, Somerville, Stoughton, Watertown, Waltham and Woburn.

The following is a summary of the Catholic churches, institutions, schools and population in the archdiocese at the close of the year 1890 :—

Churches with resident pastor . . .	122
" without resident pastor	38
" building	4
Stations attended (no church)	13
Chapels (in religious institutions)	51
Priests, secular, ...	276
Priests, regular, ...	76
Students in philosophy and theology .	97
Colleges	2
Female Academies	6
Parochial Schools	50
Convents	46
Sisters	967
Orphans asylums	10
Orphans	1,000
Hospitals	7
Number of scholars in Catholic schools, . . .	28,100
Seminary	1
Catholic population about	550,000

CATHOLIC CHURCHES IN BOSTON.

The following list of churches in the city of Boston, with their pastors and assistant priests, is taken from Hoffmann's Catholic Directory for 1891 :—

CATHEDRAL OF THE HOLY CROSS.
Most Rev. John Joseph Williams, D D.; Rev. R. Neagle, chancellor and secretary; Rev. Leo P. Boland, rector; Revs. Lawrence A. Corcoran, Henry A. Sullivan, Nicholas R. Walsh, James F. Talbot, D.D.

ST. CECILIA.
Revs. R. J. Barry, Henry A. Barry, Jno. J. Downey.

HOLY TRINITY, (German.)
Revs. F. X. Nopper, S.J., John P. M. Schlenter, S.J., Joseph Krieg, S.J.

IMMACULATE CONCEPTION.
Rev. E. J. Devitt, S.J., rector; Revs. Alphonse Charlier, S.J., P. O. Racicot, S.J., Fr. X. McCarthy, S.J., Michael J. Byrnes, S. J., Jas. Donavan, S.J., Ant. Mandalari, S.J., Jno. Buckley, S.J., Mich. Hughes, S.J., Fr. O'Neil, S.J., Jas. Collins. S.J.

ST. JAMES.
Revs. Wm. P. McQuaid, James J. O'Brien, John J. Nilan, P. H. Billings, John W. Galligan.

ST. JOHN THE BAPTIST, (Portuguese.)
Rev. Joseph Theodore de Serpa.

ST. JOSEPH, (Chamber st.)
Very. Rev. Wm. Byrne, D.D., V.G.; Revs. Thos. L. Flanagan, Edw. J. Moriarty, Wm. H. O'Connell.

ST. LEONARD OF PORT MAURICE, (Italian.)
Revs. Athanasius da Treppio, O.S.F., rector; Rev. Camillus Bonifazi, O.S.F.

ST. MARY.

Rev. Wm. H. Duncan, S.J., rector; Revs. Michael F. Byrne S.J., Fred. J. Holland, S.J., Francis Casey, S.J., Cornelius Gillespie, S.J., Augustus Langcake, S.J. Revs. Patrick J. O'Connell, S.J., and Aloysius Romano, S.J., attend city institutions on the islands. Revs. Arthur McAvoy, S.J., Fr. Barnum, S.J., Patrick Forhan, S.J., and Joseph Himmelheber, S.J., are attached to Missionary Band.

NOTRE DAME DES VICTOIRES, (French.)

Very Rev. B. Forestier, S.M., provincial; Rev. F. Coppin, S.M., rector; Rev. Anatole Police, S.M., Elphege Godin, S.M., Theophile Jos. Remy, S.M. The Marist Fathers give missions to the French Congregations.

ST. STEPHEN.

Revs. Michael Moran, John E. Hickey, B. F. Killilea, Garret J. Barry.

SACRED HEART, (Italian.)

Rev. F. Zaboglio, Miss. Ap., Guiseppe Martini, Miss. Ap., Vincenzo Astorri, Miss. Ap.

ST. PATRICK, (Boston Highlands.)

Revs. Joseph H. Gallagher, John J. Buckley, Nicholas J. Murphy, Jno. Ign. Lane.

ST. JOSEPH, (Highlands.)

Revs. Hugh P. Smyth, P.R., Arthur T. Connolly, Wm. Fennessey, Jas. J. Foley.

ST. FRANCIS DE SALES.

Revs. Patrick J. Daly, T. J. Whelan, Jno. D. Colbert, Michael J. Welch.

OUR LADY OF PERPETUAL HELP.

Rev. Jno. J. Frawley, C.SS.R., rector; Revs. Michael J. Corduke, C.SS.R., Charles Rathke, C.SS.R., Wm. O'Connor, C.SS.R., Peter Trimpel, C.SS.R., Alexander Klauder, C.SS.R., Aloysius Lutz, C.SS.R., Michael J. Sheehan, C.SS.R., Peter M. Defains, C.SS.R., Simon Grogan, C.SS.R., John Crosby, C.SS.R.

ST. AUGUSTINE, (South Boston.)

Revs. Denis O'Callaghan, John B. Halloran, Edward E. Clexton.

GATE OF HEAVEN.

Revs. Robert J. Johnson, David J. Herlihy, Patrick M. O'Connor, M. F. Murphy, N. J. Merritt.

OUR LADY OF THE ROSARY.

Revs. John J. McNulty, Denis J. Sullivan, Jas. H. McAvoy.

SS. PETER AND PAUL.

Revs. William A. Blenkinsop, M. J. Lee, Francis S. Wilson, Jno. F. James.

ST. VINCENT.

Revs. Wm. J. Corcoran, Michael J. O'Donnell, Thos. A. Walsh.

MOST HOLY REDEEMER, (East Boston.)

Revs. Lawrence P. McCarthy, Richard L. Walsh, James F. Hamilton.

OUR LADY OF THE ASSUMPTION.

Revs. Joseph H. Cassin, John J. Garrity, Thos. F. Brannan.

SACRED HEART, (East Boston.)

Revs. Michael Clarke, John S. McKone, Jno. J. Farrell.

ST. MARY STAR OF THE SEA.

Revs. Hugh R. O'Donnell, Jno. H. Griffin.

ST. CATHERINE.

Revs. Math. T. Boylan, James J. Fitzgerald.

ST. FRANCIS DE SALES, (Charlestown.)

Revs. James N. Supple, Michael J. Supple, James J. McNamara, Jno. M. Donovan.

ST. MARY, (Charlestown.)

Revs. John W. McMahon, D.D., William J. Millerick, William F. Powers.

ST. ANN. (Neponset.)

Rev. Timothy J. Murphy.

ST. PETER, (Dorchester.)

Revs. Peter Ronan, Chas. F. Glennen, Jno. W. Sullivan.

ST. GREGORY, (Dorchester.)

Revs. Wm. H. Fitzpatrick, David J. Power.

ST. THOMAS, (Jamaica Plain.)

Revs. Thomas Magennis, Philip F. Sexton, John J. Moore.

ST. COLUMBKILLE, (Brighton.)

Revs. A. I. Rossi, Fr. J. Butler, Jas. P. McGuigan.

NOTE. — The Rectors of the Cathedral, after Very Rev. P. F. Lyndon, were Rev. A. Sherwood Healy, Rev. Theodore Metcalf (*ad interim*), Rev. John B. Smith, Rev. Bernard O'Regan, Rev. Lawrence J. O'Toole, Rev. Joshue P. Bodfish, and Rev. Leo P. Boland.

CATHEDRAL OF THE HOLY CROSS.

The following description of the new Cathedral was prepared from plans of the architect, Mr. P. C. Keely, of Brooklyn, by the late Rev. A. Sherwood Healy, for the "*Cathedral*," a newspaper published during the second fair, and revised by his brother, Bishop Healy, for the third fair:—

The entire building measures over 46,000 square feet, and covers somewhat over an acre of ground. In this respect, therefore, it will take precedence of some celebrated European cathedrals; for instance, those of Strasbourg, Pisa, Salisbury, Vienna, and Venice, also St. Patrick's in Dublin. The style is early English Gothic, cruciform, with transept, nave, aisle, and clerestory, the latter being supported by two rows of clustered metal pillars, beautifully bronzed and polshed, and elegantly ornamented, which are models of grace.

The length of the church, including the Chapel of the Holy Sacrament, on the northeast corner, is 364 feet. The length of nave, exclusive of the chapel, is about 300 feet; width at the transept, 170 feet; width of nave and aisles, or of the main body of the church, 90 feet; height, to the elegant wooden ceiling, 95 feet; height, to the ridgepole, 120 feet. There are two main towers in front, and a turret, all of unequal height, and all, in time, to be surmounted by spires. The great tower, on the southwest corner, with its spire will be 300 feet in height, and the small tower, on the northwest corner, will be 200 feet. The foundations on which the larger spire will rest, are laid massive and deep, being fifty feet square, with a breadth of fifteen feet at the base.

There are no galleries, except the organ-gallery over the vestibule. The whole interior is clear space, broken only by the two rows of columns, extending along the nave, and carried to full height, as a support to the central roof. An idea of the spaciousness of the floor area may be given in saying, that the pews could accommodate from 2,500 to 3,000 persons, and, when the standing room is also occupied, about double that number could find place on this single floor.

The great organ is placed in the gallery over the front vestibule. This gallery is 40x40, and is large enough to accommodate a choir and orchestra numbering 300. On either side, and connected with it by

CATHEDRAL OF THE HOLY CROSS.

[From Photograph taken February 7, 1891.]

archways, are choral tribunes, and beyond them, in either tower, separate cloak-rooms for the gentlemen and ladies forming the choir.

The arch which separates the spacious front vestibule from the church, is built of bricks taken from the ruins of Mount Benedict.

The ceiling abounds in carved wood and tracery, and shows all the lines of a grained roof, though in light and open work, as the nature of the material and the metal supports seem to demand. The panels and spandrils show three shades of oak, with an outer line of African wood. Every alternate panel is ornamented with emblematic devices. The roof in the transept is more highly ornamented, displaying an immense cross of inlaid wood. The ceiling of the chancel is still more highly finished, for upon it are painted angels representing Faith, Hope, Charity, Temperance, and Fortitude; and clustering around in attendance, are many others, all standing out clearly and well defined on a background of gold.

The iron pillars at the transept are more massive than the others, and are each surmounted with the full-size figure of an angel. From the bands around the pillars project the numerous gas-jets by which the building is lighted.

The rose window, over the principal entrance, is, in design, a fine specimen of art. The chief glories in glass are the stained ransept windows. Each of these is 40x20 in size. The one on the southwest represents the miracle by which the true cross was verified at its finding, in 326; that opposite, the Exaltation of the Cross by the Emperor Heraclius, after its recovery from the Persians, in 629. The first of these bears the inscription, "Gift of the Confraternity of the Holy Cross." And the second, "T. and E. F. Boland, in memory of Rt. Rev. J. B. Fitzpatrick."

The central of the three windows of the chancel, over the altar, is a representation of the Crucifixion; that at the right hand, as seen from the interior of the building, represents the Resurrection, and that at the left hand, the Nativity. By the inscription placed beneath, it is made known that the first-named is a memorial window, the inscription being, "Gift of A. E. S., in memory of Bishop John B. Fitzpatrick." Inscriptions beneath the others show that they also are donations; that of the window at the right hand being, "Gift of the Very Rev. P. F. Lyndon;" and that of the window representing the Nativity, "Gift of the Rev. A. S. Healy."

Other and smaller windows are inserted in the clerestory of the transept, and of the chancel, twenty-four in number, twelve being seen at the right, and twelve at the left, from a point of view near the centre of the nave or transept. In those at the left are represented the four Prophets, Isaiah, Jeremiah, Esekiel, and Daniel; the four Evangelists, Matthew, Mark, Luke, and John; and the four great Doctors of the Church, St. Gregory, St. Jerome, St. Ambrose, and St. Augustine. The figures are full length, those of the four Doctors being within the chancel, and the others within the transept. Those of the Evangelists are accompanied by an emblematic figure, that of Matthew being an angel; of Mark, a lion; of Luke, an ox; of John, an eagle. The portraits seen at the right are those of the twelve Apostles, each of these, also, having an emblem, viz: St. Peter, the keys; St. Paul, a sword; St. Andrew, a cross; St. James, major staff and book; St. Thomas, a spear; St. James minor, a crutch: St. Philip, a gibbett; St. Bartholomew, a knife; St. Mathias, book and axe; St. Simon, a saw; St. Thaddeus, a book; St. Barnabas, rod and book.

The windows in the nave and transept are illuminated. The following is a list of their subjects, with the names of the donors:—

Epistle Side.

Mother of Mercy. Gift of Rev. Michael O'Brien.
St. Rose of Lima. Gift of Rev. James McGlew.
St. Bridget. Gift of Rev. William Halley.
St. Patrick. In memory of Patrick Treanor.
Confession of St. Thomas. In memory of Thomas Dwight.
St. Vincent de Paul. Gift of St. Vincent de Paul Society.
Mary Magdalen. Gift of Rev. A. J. Teeling.
St. Cecilia. In memory of Rev. A. Sherwood Healy.
St. Agnes. Gift of the Young Ladies' Sodality.
St. William. Gift of Patrick Denvir.

Gospel Side.

St. Augustine. Gift of Rev. J. P. Gilmore, O. S. A.
St. Francis de Sales. Gift of Rev. H. P. Smyth.
St. Thomas of Canterbury. Gift of Rev. T. B. McNulty.
St. Michael. Gift of Michael Gleason.
Memorial window of Pius IX. Gift of the Catholic Union.

St. John Baptist.   Gift of Rev. J. J. Gray.
St. John Apostle.   Gift of Revs. Michael and James Masterson.
Holy Family.   In memory of Joseph Iasigi.
St. James.   Gift of James Collins.
St. Edward.   Gift of Rev. James Ed. O'Brien.

In the large tower, the subject of the illuminated window is St. Gregory. Its donor is Rev. James O'Doherty.

There are two thicknesses of glass in each window, the outer frame containing a heavy plain glass as a protection against climatic influences.

The Sanctuary terminates in an octagonal apse, is spacious, and well adapted for the display of the splendid pageantry of pontifical rites. The High Altar is formed of rich variegated marbles, and is a masterpiece of art. Opposite it, on the left, or Gospel side, is the Episcopal throne, the *Cathedra* of the Bishop, which gives to a cathedral its name and its distinctive character.

On the right of the sanctuary and facing the south side aisle it the chapel of the Blessed Virgin, forming an octagonal recess. A rich marble altar, the gift of Tobias and the late Eleanor F. Boland, has been erected there. Above is placed a marble statue of the Blessed Virgin. Between this and the High Altar is the chapel of St. Joseph, and corresponding to this, on the left, the chapel of St. Patrick. On the left of the sanctuary, in similar position to the chapel of the Blessed Virgin, is another larger chapel for daily use, and for minor services. This is divided from the church by a transparent screen, which may at will, be removed, or rather thrown open. This chapel is known as the Chapel of the Blessed Sacrament, and is justly considered a gem of architecture. The central of the three windows in the sanctuary of this chapel, represents the Adoration of the Blessed Sacrament, and is the gift of the Most Rev. Archbishop Williams; that on the Gospel side, the Marriage of St. Joseph, and is the gift of the late Very Rev. P. F. Lyndon; and that on the Epistle, the Baptism of Our Saviour, and is the gift of P. C. Keely, architect of the Cathedral.

The large vestry is situated between the chapel of the Blessed Sacrament and the sanctuary. The chantry, with a small but handsome organ, is over the vestry, and has arches opening into the sanctuary, the Cathedral, and the Chapel of the Blessed Sacrament.

The church is thoroughly warmed by steam; the boilers are placed in the basement, two under each transept, and furnish steam for each side of the church. The heating-pipes are run along the walls under the windows and enclosed in handsome screenwork, which adds largely to the beauty of the auditorium.

The doorways to the Cathedral are five in number, and very large; three are in front, and one in each transept, so that the Cathedral, large as it is, can be emptied in a very few minutes.

THE BASEMENT OF THE CHURCH

has been arranged to the very best advantage. Under the chancel is a chapel for the children, about one hundred and twenty-five feet square, which will easily seat from one thousand to two thousand children. Here is placed *the altar of the old Cathedral in Franklin Street.* In the rear of this altar is the crypt. The boiler-rooms are also in the basement, and contain apparatus to feed over a mile of steam-piping.

There are, in the basement, eight other school-rooms, with a seating capacity of about three or four hundred each.

SILVER JUBILEE

OF THE CONSECRATION OF

ARCHBISHOP WILLIAMS.

PONTIFICAL MASS

IN THE

CATHEDRAL OF THE HOLY CROSS.

Thursday, March 12, 1891.

PONTIFICAL MASS

IN THE

CATHEDRAL OF THE HOLY CROSS.

In the whole history of the Catholic Church in Boston no event has attracted more attention among the clergy and laity than the celebration of the twenty-fifth anniversary of the consecration of the Most Rev. JOHN J. WILLIAMS, Archbishop of Boston. The services in the Cathedral of the Holy Cross on Thursday, March 12, 1891, were of the grandest and most impressive character, and were attended by the largest concourse of people ever assembled in that vast edifice. The day was one of the most beautiful of the season, and Catholics came from far and near to be present at the Jubilee Mass of their beloved Archbishop.

At half past eight o'clock, when the doors were opened, crowds of people began to pour in and soon after nine the great body of the church not reserved for pewholders was filled. The pewholders were admitted to their seats by ticket at the Union Park entrance, and before ten o'clock there was not a seat unoccupied. The aisles were then quickly filled and no standing room was reserved except a part in the centre and one side aisle for the procession to pass to and from the sanctuary. Before the services began there were at least five thousand people in the Cathedral.

At ten o'clock as the organ pealed forth the "Processional March," the head of the procession emerged from the sacristy through the Chapel of the Blessed Sacrament, passing down the aisle on the gospel side to the cross aisle, and then up the middle aisle to the sanctuary. First came the cross-bearer, censor-bearers and acolytes; next the Sanctuary Choir;

then the Seminarians from St. John Seminary, to the number of about ninety. Following them came the clergy, secular and regular, numbering over two hundred. Then came the six New England Bishops, namely:—Right Rev. M. Harkins, of Providence; Right Rev. P. T. O'Reilly, of Springfield; Rt. Rev. D. M. Bradley, of Manchester; Rt. Rev. J. A. Healy, of Portland; Rt. Rev. L. S. McMahon, of Hartford; and Rt. Rev. L. De Goesbriand of Burlington; with Bishop McQuaid, of Rochester, and Bishop Conroy of Curium. Several of the Bishops were accompanied by their Vicars General. The officers of the mass and His Grace Archbishop Wiliams closed the procession.

Pontifical High Mass was celebrated by the Archbishop, with Very Rev. William Byrne, D.D., V. G., as assistant priest; Very Rev. Mgr. P. Strain, first deacon of honor; Rev. Thos. Shahan, second deacon of honor; Rev. Leo P. Boland, deacon of the mass; and Rev. L. M. A. Corcoran, sub-deacon. Rev. James F. Talbot, D.D., was master of ceremonies, with Rev. Hugh Roe O'Donnell and Rev. George Patterson as assistants. Rev. Henry Walsh was archiepiscopal cross bearer.

The minor offices were filled as follows, by seminarians from Brighton:—Mitre, Mr. Kelleher; crozier, Mr. J. Butler; candle, Mr. O'Keefe; book, Mr. Leary; cross-bearer, Mr. O'Neill; first acolyte, Mr. Degan; second acolyte, Mr. McClean; first thurifer, Mr. McCormack; second thurifer, Mr. Lenehan; first torch-bearer, Mr. O'Malley; second torch-bearer, Mr. McCarthy; third torch-bearer, Mr. Daley; fourth torch-bearer, Mr. Holland; fifth torch-bearer, Mr. Condon; sixth torch-bearer, Mr. Sullivan.

Besides the bishops and priests who were in the Sanctuary, two rows of seats outside the railing were occupied by priests who could not be accommodated inside. It was the largest gathering of ecclesiastics ever seen in New England. The altar was decorated with lilies, roses and other exquisite flowers, and as Divine Service proceeded, the scene was one long to be remembered by those who had the privilege of being present.

After the Gospel, the Rt. Rev. James A. Healy, Bishop of Portland, delivered the following eloquent sermon:—

SERMON BY BISHOP HEALY.

But by the grace of God I am what I am, and His grace in me hath not been void; but I have labored more abundantly than all they; yet not I but the grace of God with me.—I. COR., XV. 10.

YOUR GRACE:—In this presence of Almighty God, of angels and of men; on this day and occasion, when the praises and congratulations of a great people unite with their prayers to celebrate the twenty-fifth anniversary of your consecration, it would seem more fitting to use the words of the Roman monitor to the conqueror in his triumphal procession, and to say, in the midst of this splendor and praise, "Remember thou art but man," rather than to quote the words of St. Paul, which I have taken as a text.

"I have labored more abundantly, than all they; yet not I, but the grace of God with me." But if St. Paul does in other places detail the varied phases of his apostolate, yet we can well interpret his more abundantly as appliable not to his personal merits, but to the results of his labors, which were indeed more abundant than those of any individual apostle. And in this sense, which does not conflict with that Christian humility and apostolic modesty which so well becomes you, I would, with a grateful heart, invite you, Most Rev. Brother—I would invite prelates and priests and people—to follow with me in the brief rehearsal of history, and to join with you in the hymn of praise to God, for all that His divine grace has accomplished with you and by you. In declaring, then, that you have labored more *abundantly* than all they, we may well recall who *they* were and what was the result of their labors and sacrifices.

The episcopate of Boston formally commenced with the appointment of Rev. John Cheverus as Bishop in 1808, and his consecration in Baltimore on Nov. 1, 1810.

He had fled from his beloved France, with thousands of priests, when the knife of the guillotine was their daily expectation; he had come from his refuge in England at the invitation of that saintly priest, Dr. Matignon, in 1796. Before them, Boston had seen and admired its first priest of Puritan stock, in the Rev. John Thayer, as successor to the brief ministry of two French priests, exiles from their country. Here established, the two devoted friends, Matignon and Cheverus, had labored fourteen years, when the burden of the episcopate was by request of the older priest laid upon the shoulders of the younger, and John Cheverus became the first bishop of Boston.

Dignity of rank and sublimity of order changed nothing but the outward habit of the man and the priest. A true representative of an old and honored family, he continued as a bishop the same simple manner, the same charming amiability, the same desire to be all things to all men; the same spirit of poverty, knowing, so well with the Apostle—"how to be brought low" as bishop of Boston, or "how to abound," and yet not in riches, as Cardinal-Archbishop of Bordeaux; the same zeal of an apostle that carried him repeatedly over all the vast extent of his diocese, the six states of New England.

When travelling was so slow, so difficult and wearisome, we scarcely understand how he could have accomplished so many visitations of distant colonies of Catholics without neglecting his charge in Boston. And yet, after fourteen years of priestly life and thirteen years of episcopal labors, what was the result? Great it then appeared, but admiration of the apostolic prelate yields to astonishment at present, when we consider that, after twenty-seven years, New England, in 1823, had but one priest in the city of Boston; one in Maine; one in New Hampshire; one poor little school and nine churches—buildings which could all be housed within the walls of this Cathedral; and scarcely a thousand Catholics. God does not always and to every laborer permit to see the seed-time and the harvest.

Bishop Cheverus left Boston in 1823, and on the same festival of All Saints, Nov. 1, 1825, Benedict Joseph Fenwick was consecrated the second Bishop of Boston.

He was of the race of those Catholic pilgrims of Maryland who first proclaimed and practised freedom of conscience in our country: a distinguished member of the Society of Jesus, newly risen from the ashes of its suppression. He had filled the position of president of the College at Georgetown; of pastor and missionary at New York; of an angel of peace to the divided people of Charleston, South Carolina; and he came to Boston followed by the affectionate regret of his brethren in religion and the confidence of his brethern in the episcopate. He came with a heart full of apostolic zeal, and hands full of gifts for the enlargement of his Cathedral, for the education of a clergy born in the diocese, and the promotion o christian education.

From 1825 until 1846, how wonderful would appear the history of his life, if here unfolded. Truly could he have said with the great Apostle of the Gentiles: "In journeyings often; in perils of waters, in perils of robbers; in perils from my own nation"—the scattered Catholics; in perils from the "Gentiles," the midnight convent-burner; "in perils in the city," with churches threatened by incendiaries; "in perils in the wilderness, in perils from false brethren." For twenty-one years he loved and labored; and then on the anniversary of that event (the destruction of the convent) which had saddened his remaining years, he departed from this life; not, however, without a glimpse of the land of promise. He had seen the churches increased from only one deserving the name, to forty; he had seen the harvest of priests; forty-four there were, as successor to the three who welcomed his arrival. A diocese of two fast-growing states, Connecticut and Rhode Island, set off from that of Boston under Rt. Rev. Wm. Tyler, whose name is in Benediction. But as an ardent, constant, generous, patron of Christian education, no prelate of our country surpassed him. Witness for him the ruins of the Ursuline Convent; the colony and buildings of Benedicta, in Maine. Rise up and bear witness, you sons of St. Ignatius, his brethren; rise up, students of the College of the Holy Cross, the long procession of priests and prelates, and bless his memory. Rise up, daughters of St. Vincent de Paul, Sisters of Charity; rise up with your long succession of faithful virgins and chaste matrons, your pupils, and bless the name of him who planted you in this land, as trees ladened with blessings for the generations to come. He died on the memorial August 11, 1846; but not before he had imposed hands upon his immediate successor as a Bishop of Boston, and welcomed and blessed the young priest who, after long expectation, gladdened the last months of his life, and was destined to inherit the cross and the crown as his second successor.

* * * * * *

Forty priests, forty-four churches, one college, one school, one orphan asylum — such was the condition of the Diocese of Boston when, in 1846, John Bernard Fitzpatrick became its titular Bishop. Twenty-five years, Your Grace, have indeed passed over our heads since we carried his body to its temporary resting-place in the old cemetery, among the heroes and heroines of faith of the early days of Catholicity in Boston.

And yet I can hardly speak of him as I would wish; nor can your heart more easily bear all that affectionate gratitude would move us to rehearse of that man: of majesty in presence, of breadth and depth of mind, that made his decisions of faith and rulings in morals seem like those of a Doctor of the Church — from his youth, bearing the gravity, wisdom and authority of age; a Bishop welcomed in his young manhood as a worthy compeer by the great champions of the time; for "there were giants in those days." I have but to name Hughes, McCloskey, Kenrick, Fenwick, Flaget, Rosati and England, to carry conviction to every hearer.

Such was the man in mind: but shall I say that he escaped not the common trials, crosses and sorrows of a Bishop? That would be too little. Your Grace will bear testimony that a noble, generous and loving heart, bearing most literally not only "the solicitude of all the churches" of the diocese, but the burden of many at last broke under the accumulated weight of care and suffering; and, after teaching us how to live, he taught us, who were witnesses of his last days and hours, how a bishop ought to die. In faith, in childlike piety, in blessed hope; for days and weeks listening to no word save of Eternity, when the gates opened he ascended to God; and as he departed we called after him, with our tears and sighs, "My father, my father, the chariot of Israel and the driver thereof." (IV. Kings, xi. 12.) And in answer to our cries his mantle fell upon the successor of his choice. We were witnesses twenty-five years ago; we are witnesses to-day that with his mantle of a great bishop a double portion of his spirit was given, as a double responsibility was required. Such were they, your illustrious predecessors, in this church and Diocese of Boston, worthy to be held in everlasting remembrance by men, as they will be in eternal honor before Almighty God.

But compared to the splendor of this day, this place, and this assembly, they were as those who but commence the foundations — they were as toilers in the dim aurora that precedes the day-light; they were (Heb. xi.) pilgrims . . . beholding from afar and saluting the promises that were to be realized in the coming days;

they were wise architects laying foundations, and to you, venerable brother, it has been granted to build thereon.

Twenty-five years ago, and the Diocese of Boston, of which you became the head, presented 109 churches, 119 priests, two colleges, two orphan asylums, two hospitals, three academies with 207 pupils, 5,400 pupils in eleven parochial schools and a small temporary church as pro-Cathedral.

And on this twenty-fifth anniversary, omitting the great Diocese of Springfield with its 162 priests, 107 churches, and the fifty churches and fifty-three priests of Providence Diocese, which are found in what was the then Diocese of Boston, we count 161 churches—and such churches as no other diocese of America can show; Cathedrals elsewhere can scarcely equal them; 352 priests, ninety-seven students for the priesthood. Academies, schools, convents have so increased in number that we count of academies sixteen, of convents forty-six, parochial school with nearly 30,000 pupils, 1,000 teachers, ten asylums, seven hospitals.

Truly, one might say to you, Most Reverend brother, as the prophet Isaias to the future Jerusalem: "Lift up thy eyes round and see; all these are gathered together; they are come to thee; thy sons shall come from afar, thy daughters shall rise up at thy side—then shalt thou see and abound." (ISAIAS, LX. 4.) You shall, with a heart fainting with gratitude and surprise, exclaim: It has been given to me to labor more abundantly, with more evident and more wonderful results than all they!

And here in this majestic and wide-reaching temple, the mother and mistress of the diocese, let us entone our hymn of thanksgiving. In earlier and harder days, the Cathedral was frequently the funeral monument of the Bishop that erected it. But to you it has been granted to begin and to finish, and here to display the solemn grandeur of religious ceremonial; here to assemble a great people, and here to convoke such an assembly of the clergy as we witness to-day. Here, surrounded by your brethren in the divine priesthood, like Melchisedech of old, you bless the children of the faith of Abraham; like Aaron, you offer the incense of prayer; like unto and in union with Jesus Christ, the great High Priest, you offer that sacrifice of which all others are but figures and prophecies--the Holy Sacrifice, the Immaculate Victim. "*Sanctum, sacrificium: immaculatam hostiam.*"

But what would the edifice be; what would the walls of stone, and vaults of splendor, windows of varied color and design and altars of marble; what would all be without the spirit of faith living in apostolic priests?

Count among all the blessings that have been so many and so great; count among all the wonders that it has pleased God to effect by you; count among all the varied institutions which now bless your field of labor—whether they be of tenderness for the orphan; or charity to the poor, the suffering and the aged: of rescue for the fallen, or of education in all its varied branches; count, venerable brother, the House and Sanctuary, that is, the Diocese Seminary, with its admirable teachers, where priests are formed on the model of the divine apostles, as that which should give you the greatest consolation and hope. Without the apostolic priest, the Cathedral would be a barren and silent monument. Without him, and such as he should be, the churches would be deserted; the schools worse than useless: the institutions of charity a fleeting shadow. But with a constant generation of faithful priests, the wellfare of the poor, the education of the child, the instruction and sanctification of the people, the purity and self-sacrifice of the virgin, the spread of religion, the glory of God among men, are secured unto the ages to come. Looking down as from a mountain height, I see all the extent, the order, the beauty of this camp of Israel. I see the diocese organized in every particular according to the canons of our Councils. I see the churches, the religious houses of men and women, the asylums of the sick, the aged, the tottering in virtue, the tender in age—and I exclaim: "How beautiful are thy tabernacles, O Jacob! and thy tents, O Israel! as woody valleys, as watered gardens . . . as tabernacles which the Lord hath pitched as cedars by the water side."—NUMB. xxii. 5.

But among all the trees of this Paradise there is the Tree of Life, of divine life for the priesthood. Without it all your labor was, in a measure, sterile—with it and for it you may well thank God, and cry out in wonder and gratitude: "I have labored more abundantly than all they—and yet not I, but the grace of God with me."

I feel that I should be an unworthy exponent of St. Paul's doctrine, and unfaithful representative of the emotions of your soul on this day, venerable prelate, were I to allow this assembled clergy and people to think that you attributed these wonders of God's mercy and power to yourself. "Not to us, O Lord! not to us, but to Thy Name give glory. (Ps. cxiii.) And yet not I, but the grace of God with me."

No one knows better than a bishop, no one is more frequently compelled to acknowledge that all that is done, is done by the grace of God. No one more accurately than the disciple of the Apostles measures what small part is of man's doing; and how all must be attributed to God. "Yet not I, but the grace of God with me."

When, therefore, venerable and dear brother, from whose hands all save one of your suffragan bishops have received episcopal consecration, we approach you to-day with our words of congratulation, of thanks, of praise for the past, of prayers for the future; you may welcome us to your heart of hearts. For we will express a sincere, heartfelt recognition of what it has pleased God to show forth in you, by the example of episcopal virtues, by the pre-eminent prudence, sagacity in administration, and a far-reaching wisdom that has attracted not only our admiration and affection, and that of the entire episcopate, but that of the venerable successor of St. Peter, Leo XIII., now gloriously reigning.

When your clergy approach, bearing their gifts and their words of loving gratitude, reverence and devotion, fear not to receive them. Twenty-five years' experience of an administration stamped by justice, consideration and charity, has drawn them more closely around you. From that chair you may look upon them, your army—the veterans of many a weary day and well-fought field—with grey head and bent forms, yet bringing their wreaths and their palms of their own triumphs, with the cordial buoyancy of youth—the youth of the priesthood strong in health and hope, and honors already won, press on to steady the failing hand or fill the vacant ranks—the religious orders, Oblates, Redemptorists, Jesuits, Franciscans, Augustinians, are here like the particular organizations the "*corps d'elite*" of one and the same army, bringing their tribute to the wise, considerate, and impartial leader.

Yet further away, you may see the costumes and recognize the milk-white standard of the consecrated virgins; the glory, the beauty of the Spouse of Christ; the unrivalled jewel in the crown of the Church and diocese. Receive their tribute. It is the sincerest tribute of angelic womanhood.

And with these representatives of an angelic maternity, comes the long procession of little ones; their hearts and their voices singing

Amen to all that their teachers shall utter in gratitude. After them, fear not to open wide the doors of your heart, welcome those angels of mercy, members of the conferences of St. Vincent de Paul; men of the Catholic Union, the sturdy champions of religion on every part of the field. Let the poor, whom your generosity saved from loss, approach to thank God with you, that by you they were repaid and the constant friend of the poor rescued from reproach. Fear not to welcome all; to receive all their gifts and all their praises; while they thank God for what He has done by you, you will thank God for what He has done for them, and exclaim. "Not to us, not to us Lord, but to Thy name give glory."

Amid all this manifestation of joy and thanksgiving, the very day and date intrude a sad though salutary thought. In reviewing the records of the past, I find that of all the clergy who welcomed you as a new priest in 1846, not one is living to share in the joy of this day—twenty-five years of the episcopate; forty-five years of priesthood; sixty-nine years of life. We had hardly realized that where the burden of years of labor was constantly increasing, strength and elasticity were necessarily decreasing. But while we devoutly hope and pray that he who like another Josue, will share the burdens of another Moses, may be a worthy successor to your virtues, your ability and your wisdom, we will allow ourselves to repeat to-day what the venerable Bishop, consecrating, uttered twenty-five years ago: "*Ad multos annos, ad multos annos*"—for many years, for many years may you continue to be our leader, our example; the father and model of your devoted clergy—a blessing to your people.

Ad multos annos—for many years—for many years among us: and afterwards among the saints and angels one day—the day of Eternity.

After the Benediction, the vast congregation dispersed in an orderly manner, and nothing occurred from the beginning to the end to cause the least annoyance. The arrangements in regard to the admission and seating of the people were in the hands of Mr. N. M. Williams, sexton of the Cathedral, who, with an efficient corps of ushers, made everything pass off satisfactorily.

MUSIC OF THE MASS.

The music of the Pontifical Mass was rendered by the two choirs of the Cathedral The Church Choir, augmented to two hundred voices, with organ accompaniment. Soloists: Miss Ellen A. McLaughlin, soprano; Miss Cecilia Mooney, alto; Mr. Samuel Tuckerman, tenor; Mr. John J. McCluskey, bass; Mr. Alfred De Séve, director; and Mr. J. Frank Donahoe, organist. The Sanctuary Choir, composed of seventy young men and boys, without accompaniment, instructed by M'lle G. de la Motte, Mr. C. Stumcke directing. The following was the order:—

Processional March.	Organ
Mr. J. Frank Donahoe.	
Ecce Sacerdos Magnus.	Pietro Terziani
Introit—Sacerdotes tui.	G. Capocci
Sanctuary Choir.	
Kyrie Eleison } from Messe Sollennelle. Gloria in Excelsis Deo	Gounod
Church Choir.	
Gradual—Sacredotes ejus induam Salutari. . .	G. Capocci
Tract—Beatus Vir	G. de la Motte
Sanctuary Choir.	
Veni Creator.	Cirillo
Miss Ella A. McLaughlin.	
Credo in Unum Deo—St. Cecelia Mass. .	Gounod
Church Choir.	
Offertory—Veritas Mea. . . .	. G. de la Motte
O Salutaris Hostia	. G. de la Motte
Sanctuary Choir.	
(Sanctus) { Benedictus } from Messe Sollennelle. (Agnus Dei)	. Gounod
Church Choir.	
Communion—Beatus Servius . .	. G. de la Motte
Domine Salvum fac	. . Roman
Sanctuary Choir.	
Te Deum.	. German Choral
Both Choirs.	
Viva Leone	. Gounod
The Heavens are Telling the Glory of God. .	. Haydn
Church Choir.	

The singing of both choirs was the finest ever heard in the Cathedral.

CLERGYMEN PRESENT.

Besides the Bishops aforementioned, the following clergymen were present at the Jubilee Mass:—

Rt. Rev. Mgr. Thomas Griffin, Rector of St. John's Worcester, Mass.
Very Rev. Edw. P. Allen, D D. Pres. St. Mary's Col., Emmittsburg.
Very Rev. Father Leo, O. S. F., of Belmont, N. C.
Very Rev. M. McCabe, V. G., of Providence, R. I.
Very Rev. Thomas Lynch, of Burlington, Vt.
Very Rev. John E. Barry, V. G., of Concord, N. H.
Very Rev. James Hughes, V. G., of Hartford, Conn.
Very Rev. Dr. James Powers, V. G., of Worcester, Mass.
Very Rev. J. W. Murphy, V G., Portland, Maine.
Rev. M. A. O'Kane, S. J., Pres. Holy Cross College, Worcester, Mass.

Rev. F. X. Nopper, S. J.
J. J. Frawley, C. S. S. R.
J. J. Ryan, O. S. A.
Fr. Tortel, O. M. I.
John J. Dacey. O. M. I.
Fr. Joyce, O. M. I.
E. I. Devitt, S. J.
James Doonan, S. J.
Fr. Mandalari, S. J.
Fr. Coppin, S. M.
Wm. Duncan, S. J.
Fr. Casey, S. J.
J. M. Portal, S. M.
Patrick J. Supple, D. D.
Fr. A. Cunningham.
J. B. Labossiere.
F. J. Ryan,
Wm. H. O'Connell.
John J. Ryan.
M. J. Doody.
John J. Garrity.
Martin J. Lee.
John M. Donovan.
John A. Daly.

Rev. Thomas F. Cusack.
Michael D. Murphy.
Michael Gilligan.
James McGlew.
L. J. O'Toole.
Tim. J. Danahy.
James B. Troy.
Father Athanasius, O. S. F.
R. J. Johnson.
Thomas Magennis
A. J. Rossi.
Michael Dolan.
Joseph T. De Serpa.
A. J. Teeling.
M. J. McCall.
J. E. Millerick.
Gerald Fagan.
Jno. D. Tierney.
P. J. Kavanagh.
I. P. Egan.
John M. Mulcahy.
Thomas Norris.
Tim. J. Mahoney.
M. F. Flatley.

Rev. Thomas J. Mahoney.
James F. Gilfeather.
John H. McAvoy.
Hugh J. Mulligan.
Thomas L. Flanagan.
Chas. A. O'Connor.
John P. Sullivan.
M. P. Mahon.
Denis F. Lee.
Cornelius J. Riordan.
John McGrail.
R. L. Walsh.
N. R. Walsh.
H. A. Sullivan.
R. Neagle, (chancellor).
James J. McNamara.
James Campbell.
James H. O'Neil.
Patrick B. Murphy.
Henry T. Grady,
James P. F. Kelly.
Michael J. Welch.
Jno. J. Buckley.
D. H. Riley.
Timothy J. Holland.
Thomas Walsh.
Francis J. Curran.
James Lee.
Geo. A. Rainville.
J. B. Parent.
D. J. Collins.
Chas. W. Regan.
James W. Allison.
Philip F. Sexton.
John J. Nilan
James A. Barrett.
Michael J. O'Donnell.
James J. O'Brien.

Rev. James J. Keegan.
P. J. Hally.
John O'Brien.
Wm. P. McQuaid.
Chris. T. McGrath.
J. P. Bodfish.
John W. McMahon, D. D.
P. H. Callanan.
P. J. Daly.
Michael J. Supple.
Michael O'Brien.
P. A. McKenna.
Timothy Brosnahan
Wm. E. Kelley.
John C. Harrington.
J. J. Healey.
Wm. A. Ryan.
John F. Hefferman.
John J. Gray.
P. J. Sheedy.
J. M. Guillard, O. M. I.
Thomas A. Lowney.
D. J. O'Farrell.
M. T. McManus.
Edw. L. McClure.
John Flatley.
Wm. O'Brien.
Wm. A. Blenkinsop.
Thomas Scully.
Edw. J. Murphy.
James J. Chittick.
R. P. Stack.
J. J. Murphy.
Michael F. Delaney.
John S. Cullen.
O. Boucher.
Wm. J. Corcoran.
Peter Ronan.

Rev. Daniel Gleason.
Jno. A. Donnelly.
Joseph Gadowry.
John H. Griffin.
John F. Ford.
Denis F. Sullivan.
John J. Moore.
Wm. F. Riordan.
John J. Lane.
Michael F. Murphy.
T. J. Murphy.
John E. Crowley.
Edw. J. Moriarty.
John F. Broderick.
Arthur T. Connolly.
James Gilday.
Thomas F. McManus.
John B. Galvin.
R. J. Quinlan.
Thomas J. Tobin.
D. J. Wholey.
Joseph Mohan.
Francis A. Friguglietti.
C. M. Foley.
P. Cuddihy.
Timothy Linehan.
P. J. Finnegan, (N. H.)
M. J. Corduke, C. S. S. R.
Joseph Henricks, (N. H.)
Fr. Caisse, M. A.
C. H. McKenna, O. P.
J. E. Kernan, O. P.

Rev. John F. Cummins.
B. F. Killilea.
D. O'Callaghan.
Chas. F. Glennen.
John O'Brien.
John J. Coan.
M. E. Twomey.
Jas. F. Hamilton.
L. J. Morris.
M. J. Flaherty.
James A. Walsh.
N. J. Murphy.
Francis Zaboglio, M. A.
D. J. Powers.
L. P. McCarthy.
Thomas W. Coughlin.
H. P. Smyth.
James J. Fitzgerald.
Edw. J. Curtin.
Edw. T. Schofield.
J. J. McDermott.
Father Purcell.
J. Quan.
Dr. Robinson.
Fr. Harkins.
Wm. A. Power.
R. J. Patterson.
M. Harrigan, O. P.
Fr. Renig.
John F. Kelliher.
Thos. J. Murphy.
Fr. Camillius.

Also, Rev. Father Rex, S. S. D. D., Father Chapon, S.S., Father Gigot, S. S., Father Mahoney, S. S. D. D., Father Walsh, and Father Begley, all of the Seminary.

BANQUET

IN HONOR OF

ARCHBISHOP WILLIAMS.

ADDRESS OF THE CLERGY.

Thursday, March 12, 1891.

BANQUET

AND

ADDRESS OF THE CLERGY

OF THE

ARCHDIOCESE OF BOSTON.

Immediately after the services in the church, the bishops and priests who were present at the mass assembled in the basement of the Cathedral to partake of a banquet prepared by a committee of the priests of the archdiocese in honor of His Grace the Archbishop. For the occasion, the large chapel was transformed, by the skillful arrangements of plants and evergreens, into a floral bower. Across the head was set the table for His Grace and the invited guests, from which extended five tables which accommodated two hundred and eighty priests of the diocese who gathered to take part in the exercises.

Behind the head table stood a bust of His Grace in bronze, by Kitson, draped with a purple veil, having for a background a pillar with similar draping. On the circumference in raised Roman characters, are the words "Harum, Ædium, Auctor," and on the flat surface below, engraved in the bronze, "Donum Episcoporum, Provinciæ, A.D., MDCCCXCI." This bust has since been placed in the entrance hall of the philosophical department of St. John's Seminary, Brighton.

The tables were spread in a most artistic manner by caterers J. Tyler Hicks & Co. Alongside of each plate was laid a menu card, bearing on the front the inscription, "Twenty-fifth Anniversary of the Consecration of Most Rev.

John J. Williams, D.D., Archbishop of Boston, Thursday, March 12, 1891," and surmounted by the seal of the Archbishop. On the inside was a fine line engraving of His Grace on white satin, and opposite a card containing the menu. The whole was tied with a white satin ribbon.

The post-prandial exercises were opened by Rev. J. J. Gray, who as toast-master introduced Rev. W. P. McQuaid, who read the following address to His Grace the Archbishop, from the clergy of the archdiocese of Boston, accompanied by a substantial testimonial :—

ADDRESS OF THE CLERGY.

MOST REVEREND AND BELOVED ARCHBISHOP:

The occurrence of the twenty-fifth anniversary of your consecration as Archbishop of Boston has called us together to-day to extend to you our warmest and most heartful congratulations. As priests under your immediate jurisdiction, enjoying the blessings of your fatherly care, it becomes our first duty to return thanks to the Giver of all good gifts for preserving you during all these years in the enjoyment of vigorous health, by which you have been enabled to attend in person, and without interruption, to the discharge of the onerous duties of your position. We rejoice that we behold you to-day, so little changed by the lapse of time, whose years sit so lightly upon your shoulders; and we pray that God may preserve you many years in the possession of your present activity and strength, in order that you may long continue to govern and direct us. In recalling the events of your career, we cannot fail to notice the interesting fact that your lifetime embraces every period in the history of the diocese over, which you now so happily preside.

You were born during the administration of the saintly Cheverus, our first Bishop, whose shining virtues, heroic character, and brilliant talents laid deep and strong foundations upon which Divine Providence has called you to build such a noble superstructure. You were selected as a candidate for the Priesthood by Boston's second Bishop, the illustrious Fenwick, and you served as Vicar General under our third Bishop, the profound and learned Fitzpatrick, who died happy in the knowledge that you had been appointed his successor. You were baptized in Boston's first Cathedral, you have been privileged to build, dedicate, and preside over the present one, of which Boston may well feel proud, and which easily takes rank amongst the noblest and most imposing churches of this continent. Here, too, you received at the hands of America's first Cardinal, and in the presence of the special Legate of the Holy See, the honors of the Pallium, which made you the Metropolitan of the Province of New England, and the first Archbishop of Boston. The greater part of your life has been spent in this, your native city, and it is pleasing now to recall that as you have advanced from childhood to maturer years, so you have risen from honor to honor through the successive ranks of the priestly to the episcopal, and the metropolitan dignities, and this while always remaining connected with the sanctuary of what is, in a special sense, your own Cathedral. In view of this, how well may we apply to you the words of the Psalmist, "The just shall flourish like the palm tree, he shall grow up like the cedar of Libanus." "They that are planted in the house of the Lord shall flourish in the courts of the house of our God." Ps. xci 13, 14.

It is unnecessary to enumerate all the changes that have taken place in the diocese since it was first placed under your jurisdiction. Though considerably diminished in territory by the erection of the Sees of Springfield and Providence, it has steadily advanced in every department of parochial and diocesan equipments. A comparison of the Catholic Directories for 1866 and 1891 reveals a progress most astonishing in its contrasts, and most suggestive in its various details, while it indicates a prosperity which forms the most substantial tribute to your unremitting energy and well-directed zeal. Year after year churches have arisen as if by magic in every town and village, so that, to-day, there is no community of Catholics in any portion of the diocese that has not a suitable place of worship within easy reach. In recent years, especially, schools have multiplied in all the chief centres of population, and with the introduction of the numerous Sisterhoods and Brotherhoods, especially devoted to teaching, a large proportion of the children of the diocese now enjoy the inestimable blessing of a good Catholic education. Asylums, hospitals, and other charitable institutions which scarcely existed at all twenty-five years ago, have since been established in all of our principal cities, and there is, at present, hardly a class of the unfortunate or destitute amongst us which is not suitably provided for in large and well equipped homes. It is gratifying to note here, in connection with the work of providing for the poor, that you enjoy the honor of having established the first Conference of St. Vincent de Paul in the diocese, and all who have had experience of the working of that splendid organization of Catholic charity, as it exists in so many of our parishes at this hour, can appreciate the vast amount of good that has been accomplished by the introduction of such an efficient and wisely adjusted means of providing for the victims of want and misfortune.

The religious orders and societies which everywhere form such an influential factor in church work, have always received from you special encouragement, and there is no portion of the diocese which represents a larger growth in the past, or holds forth brighter prospects for the future.

Among the latest of your works, and which deserves special mention is the Seminary of St. John, which stands to-day, completed as it is pre-eminent among the educational establishments of the land, a credit to your zeal, and an honor to the diocese, securing for the future, the perpetuation of what is most special and important in the work of the Church, a devoted and zealous priesthood.

Some idea of the part you have taken in the building up of the diocese may be formed from the fact, that, of the three hundred and fifty priests now within your jurisdiction, only twenty were in holy orders at the beginning of your administration, and of the one hundred and twenty-four pastors now in the diocese, all but three have received their present appointments from you.

The population of the diocese during this quarter of a century, from two hundred thousand to more than half a million, is made up of a people distinguished for their fidelity to religious duty, their zeal in all good works, and their generosity in answering every appeal of religion and humanity.

There is no people of stronger faith or more open-handed charity, and on the other hand, owing to the splendid ecclesiastical organization which you have established, there is no people whose spiritual needs are better supplied or more faithfully guarded.

It must be extremely gratifying to you to look back over these twenty-five years, and witness this remarkable growth and advancement, and to reflect that all this has been brought about under your guiding influence. Moreover, though Boston as a city, notwithstanding her great increase in population, has been outstripped by other cities in the country, Boston, as a Catholic diocese, still holds a front rank among the dioceses of the United States, and in some respects she is proud to claim even the first place.

But our special interest to-day is with you individually, and whatever may be the material increase and prosperity of the diocese, and whatever honor it may have acquired for itself, or conferred upon you, all this becomes of secondary importance when we turn to consider the hold which you have on the hearts of your priests, and the place you occupy in their esteem and affection.

These cannot be measured by figures or lines, but as in the lapse of time each year has given us new proofs of your wisdom, your cautious forethought, your patient forbearance, and your uniform fairness in all your dealings with us, so each year has developed in our hearts renewed love and regard for you personally, an ever stronger loyalty to your official authority, and an ever increasing admiration for your noble character.

Your rule, always firm but gentle, has been pre-eminent for justice, impartiality, and kindness; and while an admirable prudence has always characterized your general administration of affairs, you have at all times, so identified yourself with our individual interests, and so warmly espoused our personal projects, that each and every one of us has been led to look upon you as his special friend and well wisher, and the authority of the superior being held in abeyance, we remember only the kindly tenderness of the father, and what can best be likened to the affectionate goodwill of the companion and associate. Nor can we forget to-day your many charities, hidden indeed from the world, and done in silence, yet being so numerous and widespread, they cannot remain entirely unknown. Their very silence and secrecy proclaim them to be the special promptings of the heart and the best proof of a generous and unselfish nature. The memories of twenty-five years are crowded with evidences of your admirable tact and discretion in the management of this large and important diocese. Especially has this been manifested in the recent display of sectarian bigotry of which our city has been the unfortunate witness. In this you have given proof of a temper so well under control, and a wisdom so far-seeing, that we have been forced to admire your patience under circumstances so apt to exasperate, and we feel bound to congratulate both you and ourselves on your firm adherence to a course difficult indeed to most men, but so much in harmony with Christian charity and the soundest policy, and already vindicated by results in the assured and inevitable triumph of the right.

We have long learned to look upon you as our pattern and model in the clerical life. The order and system that have ever characterized the discharge of your official duties, the fidelity to trust, the promptness and accuracy of method which have ever accompanied your business relations, conspicuous as they are, are no more admirable than the sincere and unobtrusive piety by which you have constantly edified both priests and people under your charge. Your judgments have always commanded respect for their soundness, and your decisions have always gone without appeal, so that the Judges of Ecclesiastical Causes, both here and at Rome, might with great propriety to-day be presented with white gloves, as nothing has been referred to them from Boston. This fact alone is the best evidence of your wisdom, integrity and fairness.

We have been glad, moreover, to find that these admirable attributes of mind and character have been as fully appreciated abroad as at home, and that both in the Councils of the National Church at Baltimore, and of the Universal Church at Rome, you have been looked up to, deservedly, as a prudent and wise counsellor, and your judgment in matters of discipline and administration has been respected and adopted as the wisest and best in practise.

On all these occasions, too, we have been gratified to learn that you have ever kept a watchful guard over the interests of your priests, and made their cause your own, so using your influence as to secure legislation advantageous to the humblest as well as to the most favored in the ranks of the clergy. This has ever been the characteristic of your administration, and in those cases where you have been obliged to pass censure, no one has found cause for complaint, for in the exercise of authority you have always seasoned justice with mercy.

With abundant reason, therefore, do we approach you on this happy occasion, to tender you our most earnest and sincere congratulations. In testimony of our cordial affection and deep veneration, we beg of you to accept this offering. It is a personal gift direct from the hearts of all the priests of this archdiocese. We come, therefore, to-day, with a profound sense of duty, urged on by gratitude and love, to proclaim our admiration for your splendid achievements, our appreciation of your many grand and estimable qualities, our acknowledgment of your many acts of kindness and generous consideration, and our hearty felicitations on the completion of a glorious quarter century of an episcopate forever memorable in the annals of the American Church.

THE CLERGY OF THE ARCHDIOCESE
OF BOSTON.

The Archbishop, in a few well chosen words, full of emotion, made his response of thanks.

The toasts were then read and responded to as follows:—

"*Our Holy Father Leo XIII.*" Responded to by Rt. Rev. Louis de Goesbriand, (who in behalf of the Bishops presented to the Archbishop the bust before described.)

"*The Bishops of the Province.*" Responded to by Bishop O'Reilly.

"*Our Invited Guests.*" Responded to by Bishop McQuaid and Bishop Conroy of New York.

"*Clergy of the Archdiocese.*" Responded to by Fathers Shahan and Blenkinsop.

Following the toasts, His Grace briefly addressed the clergy an l the gathering dispersed.

SILVER JUBILEE RECEPTION

IN HONOR OF THE CONSECRATION OF

MOST REV. JOHN J. WILLIAMS, D. D.

BY THE

CATHOLIC UNION OF BOSTON,

AT THE

BOSTON COLLEGE HALL,

ON

THURSDAY EVENING, MARCH 12, 1891.

CATHOLIC UNION PROGRAMME.

Committee of Arrangements.

THE EXECUTIVE COMMITTEE OF THE UNION.

THOMAS B. FITZ, *President.*
JOHN W. MCDONALD, *1st Vice-President.*
JAMES A. REILLY, *2d Vice-President.*
JOHN J. MCCLUSKEY, *Rec.-Sec. and Treas.*
THOMAS J. KELLY, *Cor.-Secretary.*
THOMAS A. CRAWFORD.   DANIEL L. PRENDERGAST,
FRANCIS MARTIN,   STEPHEN MURPHY,
J. B. FITZPATRICK.
REV. LEO P. BOLAND, - - - - - - *Spiritual Adviser.*

Honorary Committee.

EX-PRESIDENTS.

THEODORE METCALF.   JOHN B. MORAN, M.D.
HON. HUGH O'BRIEN.   J. AUDLEY MAXWELL.
THOMAS DWIGHT, M.D.   THOMAS F. RING.
JOSEPH D. FALLON.   JAMES L. WALSH.

Ushers.

D. L. PRENDERGAST.

Thomas J. Kelly,		John D. Berran,
Chas. F. Kelly,	Jas. J. McCluskey,	D. H. Mahony,
H. V. Cunningham,	Hubert J. McLaughlin,	John W. Mitchell,
J. J. Linehan,	F. J. McLaughlin,	E. A. Paige,
John A. Bruen,	James H. Carney,	Fred C. Dowd,
F. E. McWiggin,	Geo. C. Keenan,	James L. Corr,
F. L. Cadogan,	Wm. P. Cashman,	John B. Whelton,
F. E. Donohoe,	Geo. M. Cranitch,	Frank T. Mara,
Peter J. Finnigan,	Chas. J. Gorman,	Geo. McCarthy,
Hugh Mullen,	Chas. D. Murphy,	Frank A. Campbell,
Jos. A. Ryan,	W. H. Fernekees,	John D. O'Connor.

Order of Exercises.

March. Jubilee, . . . *Boeckelmann*
>ORCHESTRA.

Gloria in Excelsis Deo, from 12th Mass. *Mozart*
>BOUQUET OF ARTISTS.

Largo, ... *Handel*
>ORCHESTRA. (Violin obligato by Mr. John C. Mullaly.)

Addresses to the MOST REV. ARCHBISHOP.
>President THOMAS B. FITZ.
>THOMAS J. GARGAN, Esq.

Domine Saluum fac . . *Roman*
>CHOIR.

Response of
>Most Rev. JOHN J. WILLIAMS, D. D.

Hymn to the Pope. Viva Leone, *Gounod*
>CHOIR.

Overture. "Wm. Tell," . . *Rossini*
>ORCHESTRA.

National Hymn. To thee, O Country. *Julius Eichburg*
>CHOIR.

Order of Exercises.

Jubilee Ode, written for the occasion by *Mary Elizabeth Blake*
MR. THOMAS A. MULLEN.

Hallelujah Chorus,   *Handel*
CHOIR.

Divertisement Espagnol.   *Desormes*
Bolero, Havanaise, Cachucha, Zapateado.
ORCHESTRA.

Te Deum,   *German Choral*
Choir and audience standing.

TE DEUM.

Holy God, we praise thy name!
Lord of all, we bow before Thee.
All on earth thy sceptre claim,
All in Heaven above adore Thee;
Infinite Thy vast domain;
Everlasting is Thy name.

Hark! the loud celestial hymn,
Angel choirs above are singing;
Cherubim and Seraphim,
In unceasing chorus praising;
Fill the Heavens with sweet accord;
Holy! Holy! Holy Lord!

Thou art King of Glory, Christ!
Son of God, yet born of Mary,
For us sinners sacrificed;
And to death a tributary,
First to break the bars of death,
Thou hast opened Heaven to Faith.

✳—ARTISTS.—✳

Representing Fifteen Church Choirs.

SOPRANOS.

Miss Lizzie Clahane,
Miss Mamie Crowley,
Mrs. Frank P. Ewing,
Mrs. Ellen Farricey,
Mrs. Julia Dorgan Herrick,
Miss Nellie Kinnahan,
Miss Kate A. Mahoney,
Miss Ellie M. McCarthy,
Miss Ellen A. McLaughlin,
Mrs. Josie Mooney,
Mrs. Ella J. O'Donnell,
Miss Annie Pieper,
Miss Mildred E. Tuckerman,
Miss Kate M. Reilly,
Miss Anna C. Westervelt.

ALTOS.

Miss M. Agnese Conroy,
Miss Annie Curley,
Mrs. Ita Welsh Donovan,
Miss Theresa Flynn,
Miss Annie T. Gaffney,
Mrs. T. H. Holohan,
Mrs. T. H. Keenan,
Miss Mary E. McCarthy,
Miss B. E. McLaughlin,
Miss Teresa Maginnis,
Mrs. Annette McMunn,
Miss Anna Mennig,
Miss Nellie Moore,
Miss Cecelia Mooney,
Miss Mary Mulvey,
Miss Carrie Reid.

TENORS.

Mr. D. C. Dillworth,
Mr. J. B. Donovan,
Mr. M. J. Dwyer,
Mr. F. P. Ewing,
Mr. James J. Maloney,
Mr. Eugene F. McCarthy,
Mr. P. A. McLaughlin,
Mr. R. McMunn,
Mr. J. F. Sheehan,
Mr. Samuel Tuckerman,
Mr. A. A. Turner,
Mr. Jas. F. Woods.

BASSOS.

Mr. R. J. Brooks,
Mr. Henry Canning,
Mr. Jno. H. Carroll,
Mr. Thos. E. Clifford,
Mr. Geo. B. Crosby,
Mr. Martin F. Curley,
Mr. Charles T. Dolan,
Mr. Frank Donnelly,
Mr. Wm. J. Finnigan,
Mr. Jno. E. Gilman,
Mr. John J. McCluskey,
Mr. Frank P. O'Connor,
Mr. Jno. D. O'Connor,
Mr. Thos. F. Ryan,
Mr. Jno. A. Tobin.

SELECTED ORCHESTRA.

Twenty-two Members of the Boston Symphony Orchestra.

Choir and Orchestra under the direction of Mr. JOHN C. MULLALY.

J. Frank Donahoe and James T. Whelan, Accompanists at Rehearsals.

RECEPTION

IN HONOR OF

ARCHBISHOP WILLIAMS,

BY THE

CATHOLIC UNION OF BOSTON.

The reception given by the Catholic Union to His Grace the Archbishop was, next to the grand solemn services at the Cathedral, the most notable feature of the Silver Jubilee celebration. The Union has given many brilliant receptions to distinguished clergymen and prelates since its organization, but this last one to its Most Rev. Honorary President and founder, on the evening of the twelfth of March, 1891, excelled all previous efforts. The spacious new hall of Boston College was generously placed at the disposal of the Union by the rector, Rev. Father Devitt. S. J., and no more suitable place in Boston could have been selected. The decorations were in keeping with the grand event. Streamers of red, white and blue alternated with evergreen were hung from the ceiling and festooned on the walls. Over the front of the stage was a dome from which draperies of white satin hung gracefully to the sides, and were caught up by shields bearing the dates "1866," "1891." Connecting these was a silver chain of twenty-five links. The whole effect was simple, yet suggestive and elegant, and showed the artistic skill of Brother Fealy of the College. The front of the stage was banked with a profusion of superb lilies and other potted plants from the conservatory of Galvin Bros.

Before the opening of the exercises, every seat in the hall

was filled by Union members and their friends, to the number of about sixteen hundred, and when the audience rose in honor of the Archbishop, bishops and clergymen, as they were escorted through the middle aisle to their seats on the stage, the scene was inspiring beyond description. First came the ushers wearing purple badges across their breasts, then the honorary committee and government with the clergymen and bishops, and then the president with the Archbishop. While the procession moved, the orchestra played the Jubilee March, and after the guests were seated, "Gloria in Excelsis Deo" from Mozart's 12th Mass was given with magnificent effect by the bouquet of artists. After another fine piece of music by the orchestra, the President of the Union, Mr. Thomas B. Fitz, addressed the Archbishop as follows:—

PRESIDENT FITZ'S ADDRESS.

Your Grace, Right Reverend and Reverend Clergy, Members of the Catholic Union, Ladies and Gentlemen—In behalf of the Catholic Union, which I have the honor to represent, my first and pleasant duty to-night will be to congratulate Your Grace on this the glorious event of your jubilee.

In doing so we know that our hearts and our voices are simply re-echoing the filial and affectionate sentiment lovingly breathed forth for you at this time not only by hundreds of thousands of Catholics in your archdiocese and throughout the country, but by the entire community, which has so long witnessed the beneficence of your ministrations and the healthful influence of your uncompromising personality.

The Catholic Union welcomes most cordially the bishops and reverend clergy, and the ladies and gentlemen present who have come here to mingle their salutations with ours, and our only regret is the incapacity of any possible place of meeting which would adequately accommodate the thousands who would feel honored with the opportunity of presenting to you their heartfelt good wishes to-night.

It is truly a glad and joyous occasion for us to be permitted the privilege of joining in that universal anthem of praise and thanksgiving which has gone forth to-day from altar and sanctuary, from religious community and humble home, all blessing the goodness of God for preserving your life and health to celebrate this event. Apart, however, from the tender personal sentiments and loving memories which hallow this day, we are not unmindful of its more serious significance in representing a most important milestone in the history of Catholicity in New England.

The term of your episcopacy is synonymous with the traditions of the Catholic Church in the East for a quarter of a century. Every act of yours is irrevocably linked with that chain of events which not only gives testimony of your zeal and wise direction, but also symbolizes the authority of your mission and the vitality of our holy religion. Thus a thousand memories of your paternal devotion to the spiritual and temporal welfare of the people have been reflected by the advent of this day, prompting us to present to you personally the humble tribute of our affection and gratitude, and to your sacred office the testimony of an unflinching fidelity and admiration.

Am I not right then, ladies and gentlemen, in saying that there is no attachment, no devotion, no admiration, like unto that cherished by a dutiful people toward a faithful steward, whose unselfish interest and unremitting labors are sanctified by the seal of spiritual authority? I am not unmindful, however, that in presiding at this meeting it is neither my province nor my purpose to review even incidentally the labors and ministrations of His Grace our beloved Archbishop. Whatever may be said in this way is fittingly left to one whose genius and eloquence will do more justice to such a privilege.

I know, however, that the generous patronage extended by His Grace towards the Catholic Union, from its very inception to the present day, entitles me to say a special word in its behalf, in recognition of this kindly interest and in pledge of our continued obligations to him. You, fellow-members of the Catholic Union, know that I simply bespeak your sentiments when I say that largely to his active interest, to his encouraging words and wise counsel are we indebted for the success of our association and its representative character in our Catholic community.

I wish, gentlemen of the Union, that I could do you and myself the justice of adequately expressing the depth of gratitude we feel accordingly, and the earnestness of our purpose to merit a continuance of this favored confidence in future. I believe, however, that His Grace will accept this candid protestation, measuring it by the sincerity of its expression, rather than by the humble language in which it is couched.

Knowing the desire of the Archbishop that our Union should be representative in deeds as well as in name, I am justified in the assumption that there is no tribute of thanks we could offer him that would be so acceptable as the assurance that the aim and efforts of the Union will be pledged to a continued correspondence with those high principles which unite Catholic laymen in bonds of brotherhood like this, to co-operate with their clergy in upholding Catholic interests and ennobling their manhood by works of charity and usefulness towards their fellow-men.

The largely increased membership of the Catholic Union and the introduction of several new and important features of work in the last few years afford ample proof of its intention to merit a claim to such a position in our community. That it holds such a place is, as I stated before, largely due to the active assistance and encouragement given by Your Grace.

It is useless, however, to single out this, or any one of the works in which you have taken such on active interest, as an evidence of your zeal, for they all bear the impress of your devotion to the spiritual and temporal good of the people, and not only prompt festivities coincident with a jubilee like this, and the prayers of the faithful that many, many years of life and health may be spared to you, but eloquently assert your claim to an affectionate and imperishable remembrance for a long, long time to come.

After his address, Mr. Fitz introduced the Hon. Thomas J. Gargan, who discoursed as follows:—

MR. GARGAN'S ADDRESS.

May it please Your Grace and Ladies and Gentlemen of the Catholic Union of Boston — Rich in fitting voices competent to speak on this occasion, the modesty of my fellow-members of the Catholic Union has impelled them to invite me to perform what would be a most pleasing and agreeable duty could I find words to give adequate expression to the ardor which stirs their hearts on this anniversary.

Twenty-five years of self-sacrificing service! How long a time it seems to the young looking forward, yet how brief to those looking backward. In that long, bright retrospect, I believe I am warranted in saying your Catholic and non-Catholic fellow-citizens rejoice and thank God for this quarter of a century of your episcopacy.

With joyful hearts we congratulate you on this most happy day of your jubilee. We offer our humble tribute of thanksgiving and praise for what you have done for us and what you have been to us.

Many of us in this audience to-night have followed with tender interest your career as priest, bishop and archbishop, and, while we are deeply grateful that His Holiness has honored you by conferring upon you the well-merited dignities of bishop and archbishop, yet I am sure that many of us of your earlier congregations, who remember you at the old Cathedral on Franklin street, at the chapel on Beach street and at the chapel at the West End, have so enshrined you in our hearts that no honors nor dignities conferred upon you can make you more deeply revered or dearer in our eyes than you were as Father Williams. Where, indeed, may one begin in our field of deep rejoicing?

We feel indebted to you for sound instruction, good advice, wise counsel and safe guidance in every way. We remember the exactness with which you performed the many duties of your holy ministry, your earnestness, your charity, your love for the little ones and for God's poor and your devotion to the sick and the suffering.

We remember your promotion to the vicar-generalship of the diocese, your assignment to the pastorate of the old church of St. James on Albany street, your almost herculean labors to relieve the parish from its enormous debt. The same modesty and firmness that marked your earlier career as a priest distinguished you as a vicar-general, and when, in the fullness of time, it pleased God to call you to be bishop of the diocese of Boston, the clergy and laity rejoiced with unexampled enthusiasm and satisfaction. What changes have taken place since March 12, 1866! Then the whole Catholic population of the Commonwealth of Massachusetts was under your administration, and I think I then knew by sight and by name every priest in the diocese. Since your consecration as bishop the diocese of Springfield and a large part of the diocese of Providence have been set off; yet to-day the archdiocese has 160 churches, more than 300 priests and 30,000 children in its parochial schools. Many of these churches are out of debt thanks to your wise financial management.

Convents, houses for the orphans and destitute children and for the aged poor have been established, and the magnificent cathedral has been erected, under your supervision.

In the advancement of the higher education, you have given us St. John's Seminary at Brighton, and you have contributed largely to the establishment of the new Catholic University at Washington, all for "the glory of the Creator and the relief of man's estate." These twenty-five years have been to you years full of toil and anxiety for the Catholic church and Catholic people.

Grave questions have arisen requiring the most patient investigation and the exercise of the greatest discretion to decide aright. You have had a partial reward in the approval of your own conscience and in the respect of all in the archdiocese, who acknowledge you as their universal parish priest.

Your brethren of the clergy, fellow-soldiers with you in the great battle for christianity, can most fully appreciate your eminent services to the Church; as laymen, we do not forget the part you had in the great Vatican Council, convened in 1869 and 1870, where the subject of Papal Infallibility was long and earnestly debated by the most learned theologians of the Church.

We recall the wisdom with which you and other American bishops approved the decision that on the question of faith and morals our Holy Father the Pope was the supreme judicial judge, from whose decision there was no appeal. We remember with pride and satisfaction your eminent services in the plenary councils at Baltimore; and living, as we do, in a community where a large part of the population look with a jealous and hostile eye on the Catholic church and the Catholic clergy, and knowing that during your ministry they have been scorned and derided, we cannot be niggard in our praise when we think of the wisdom of your course and the success of your efforts in so firmly establishing the Catholic church in New England. "We should not only praise, but hasten to praise," to quote Sir Robert Walpole.

It is admitted by all thinking men that the impelling and controlling force in our modern civilization is christianity. The wise statesman recognizes the necessity of religion for the preservation of the State; he knows that without religion the result must be communism, anarchy, nihilism.

The sound thinker knows it must be a religion founded on authority; he recognizes the necessity of authority in every department of the civil government, and the necessity of an authority that shall be supreme. Under our republican form of government we have first the authority of a written constitution, under which the people elect their legislature and executive, yet above and beyond all this is our very safeguard, the Supreme Court, to interpret the laws and to expound the constitution with authoritative voice.

You have maintained during your career the necessity of a properly constituted authority in the government of the state as in the government of the church. When the church speaks on the question of faith and morals she speaks with the voice of authority; yet we of the faith know her to be the most democratic institution in the world. She knows no color nor caste nor country; the humblest of her sons may aspire to the priesthood and to her highest honors.

Under the teaching and training of the church, Catholics ought to be good citizens. We know that they are when they live up to the precepts of the church, and, while we are here to-night to give expression to our veneration for you as our beloved archbishop, we do not forget you are our fellow citizen; that Boston is the city of your birth; that your infant feet first trod the streets of this city which you love so well; here you have lived and walked in and out among us, boy and man, for more than three score years.

We know your devotion to her people and to her interests, and we know of your fidelity to the constitution and the laws of your country. You have never held public office nor participated in the strife of party politics, and we do not even know to what political party you belong; yet I know of no man more influential than yourself in the community in which you live.

On all the great questions that have agitated the country and affected the rights of humanity, when you have spoken, your voice has been potent, because it has been uplifted in the cause of truth and of universal justice. Since your ordination to the priesthood, and your consecration as bishop, there have been some troublous times in Massachusetts.

You witnessed a great wave of fanaticism sweep over us when the mob spirit was invoked, and agitators paraded and harangued crowds upon the Lord's day. You saw our churches threatened with destruction, our Catholic institutions of piety and learning ruthlessly invaded by committees under the forms of law, and it seemed as though the Catholics had borne with every indignity. They had been smitten on the right cheek and turned the other also to receive a more stinging blow. Their forbearance was almost exhausted.

In those trying times you preserved a calm and firm demeanor, counselling patience sufficient to wait for the sober second thought of the people. Who can estimate the power of your influence for the preservation of law and order with the people, wrought to the highest pitch of indignation at what they believed, and what they knew, to be the violation of their civil and religious rights.

In the agitations and conflicts between labor and capital in this State, when at times men were collected like heaps of tinder and demagogues so vigorously striking flint and steel that conflagration seemed imminent, your sympathies were ever on the side of the oppressed. You believed that the employer had a grave responsibility and a christian duty to perform toward the employee. But your influence was against all forcible and rash measures.

You believed the law of the land ought to be obeyed, that justice would finally right many wrongs. Your course in this archdiocese has made you a great conservative force. We know you do not covet worldly honors, yet, if your fellow-citizens were called upon to select a man who, in their judgment, had contributed as much as any other to the peace and prosperity of this community, I believe that Most Rev. John J. Williams would be selected.

I pause here with a heart overflowing, not knowing where to end. I have left unsaid many things I would wish to have said, if Your Grace were not present. We remember and speak with fitting reverence of the blessed dead; of your predecessors, Cheverus, Fenwick, and Fitzpatrick. In their day and time they did grand work and achieved much for the church and diocese of Boston, but to you came a broader field and greater responsibilities.

"New occasions teach new duties." You have always risen to the level of the occasion, and we bear testimony that all new duties have been courageously met. We have known you in your years of service to be modest, generous, just and self-denying. In all things the noble character, the exalted citizen, the model priest.

Speaking as I do here tonight for the members of the Catholic Union — for its enthusiastic ladies no less than for the gentlemen — I have the honor, Your Grace, to formally tender you, on the 25th anniversary of your episcopacy, the heartiest congratulations and best wishes for health and happiness.

As I look about in the audience to-night and note the youthful faces, eager eyes so brave with the certainty of the future, I may be pardoned if I cannot repress a pang of envy, or at least regret, that some of us may not stand in our places, as now we do to call down blessings on your head when the great day arrives of your golden jubilee. To you, the young people of to-day, the privilege will descend.

My brethren of the Catholic Union, I think as I see you before me, would we exchange places? Ah, hardly would we give up the treasured memory of his grand young manhood, no more deeply absorbed in the sacredness of his calling now than he was then; all of the long array of his unusual deeds of mercy and charity and wisdom. Who that has ever needed can forget the gracious tenderness of his kindness, indeed all the high virtues that contribute to the perfect prelate? No, we of the older ones will hold to the past dear remembrances, still deeply loving in our hearts our noble Archbishop, glorying in his record, proud to be numbered among his flock—the good shepherd, indeed, whose very face is a benediction.

Mr. Gargan's address was listened to with close attention and warmly applauded. "Domine Salvum Fac" was then sung by the choir.

When the Archbishop stepped forward to reply the audience arose and gave him a most enthusiastic greeting, and while he stood waiting for the applause to cease it could be seen that he was deeply affected. He spoke without notes of any kind, and all who heard him felt that his words came from the fullness of his heart. Never before was he more truly eloquent, yet as simple and direct as a father talking to his children.

He was emphatically in earnest, and his address will be accepted as an inspired utterance.

ADDRESS OF ARCHBISHOP WILLIAMS.

Mr. President of the Union, and Ladies and Gentlemen:

If at other times I were prepared to express my feelings on an occasion like this, it would be impossible for me to do so after the excitement of this day. I should like to give words that would express my satisfaction at this ovation presented to me on my twenty-fifth anniversary. When I look back over the last few days I see how this has been accumulating. Although I knew it was to come, and the day was appointed, yet I was not aware of the feelings it would produce in the community, and it is only gradually that the interest you take in the anniversary of him who is at the head of your diocese dawned upon me; for, although so much is addressed to me personally, still I have, in spite of all the praise I have received, coolness enough to distinguish and to know perfectly well how much is due to my position, and how little belongs to myself personally. I have been placed in a position where I was observed by all, where I had to take the lead in many things. Had I not been there, another would have done the work, and why not as well, if not better, than I have.. I feel like one who has charge of a vessel. There are numbers of men aboard who work, one for one purpose and another for another purpose. He who guides the vessel has the whole credit, and still he but represents the whole. And so it is with him at the head of the diocese. If I have done anything for which I should take credit to myself, it is, as I say, owing to my clergy, and also to the laity. I have simply to hold the rudder strongly, give the vessel the right direction, and the winds and waves will carry it where I wish it to go. They simply require a hand to guide them and to restrain them. There is plenty of will and plenty of energy, and the duty of him who is at the helm is to see that they are directed in the right manner. I feel somewhat in this position, so that I am not vain enough to apply to myself all the flattering things that have been said during this day. But I can appreciate the affection, the respect, and the pleasure that people show on this day of my anniversary, and I should be too glad to-night to be able to make you feel what joy it has given me to see the community filled with the pleasure of the day, not only on my account, but on the account of the position which I hold.

My affection is for Boston, of course — like all souls that are filled with the proper spirit, the birthplace comes before any other part of the earth — and were it less than it is I should still be proud of it. And when it comes to speaking of Boston, I have no reason to be ashamed of it for anything, and certainly I have no reason to be ashamed of it for the Catholic portion. From the beginning to the present, the Bishops who were here received consolation from their people. They had their people's confidence and their respect; they deserved it fully; and they received it. And since I have been here for twenty-five years it has never been wanting whenever there was an opportunity to show it. The gentleman who spoke alluded to the times that have passed over us; unpleasant times, not those of olden years before my time of episcopacy. I allude especially to those of the last years, when so much was done to irritate the Catholics of Boston, so much was done to insult them, so much was done to make them revolt against all their principles, and not turn the left cheek wher the right was struck. Yet they remained firm, and to-night here in this great assemblage, on this day of the anniversary. I am glad to say publicly that I am proud of the Catholics of Boston for the last two years. It is not the accusations that were made against us, not the revilings even, not even the insults, that I find fault with, but the attacks which were made on the virtue of our ladies in religious societies. The revilers attacked the clergy, but to that we were less sensitive, because we are men. But when they attacked women who had devoted their lives to virginity, spouses of Christ, and kept up the attack; when placards were placed on our walls and not torn down by the authorities of the city—then it was almost time to resent the injuries. And yet you remained quiet. For this I give you credit, and for this I am proud to-day. It was a time, indeed, for every one to mutter and gnash his teeth as he went through the streets.

For myself, I knew the trouble came not from the better part of the community. It was only a storm that was passing over. What irritated me—and I will give vent to it to-night—was not the insults, nor the accusations, nor the revilings, but I was ashamed of Boston that all these did not commence with those who expressed them openly: they came in cold blood for politics. And you, gentlemen, who look back will see—and they will see—that before a certain time not long ago we were quiet. From time to time some individual would write a book or publish a pamphlet, or put something in a paper about the Catholics, but it was only the transient. The persistent abuse came in consequence of this plot to make use of the attack on Catholics and their schools for a political election. This is the truth. And it was only afterwards, when these politicians cared no more for it, when they had gained their point and had dropped it and were willing to have it lost for them, that others took it up and made use of it. From the first spark came the great illumination from these gentlemen against the Church. I was ashamed, not of the last, but of the first. I think the politicians of that class who were willing to set the city and the country on fire for a small election in the State will look back and be ashamed of it, when they consider that were it not for the determination of Catholics not to be driven into anything against the law—on account of the firmness of Catholics who are not willing to give way to that feeling of revenge or irritation— that were it not for them, no one can tell what would have been the consequences. And when we know that if one-tenth of what had been said and done against us in the last two years had been said and done by us against any sect in the city or country, it would not be twenty-four hours before there would be bloodshed. They have reason to be ashamed. It is only because we have something stronger than mere sentiment, that we restrained ourselves. Whilst the revilings were passing away we felt that our faith was not hurt, no harm was really done, and we knew that the effect of it all would be to strengthen us, to bring us closer together, shoulder to shoulder, against those who would hurt us, and that the respectable part of the community would join with us after the storm had passed over. We knew perfectly well that the better portion of the community was not with these revilers. But what we have against those gentlemen — those conservative gentlemen, who would not mix in such business — is that, whilst they condemned it and whilst they were too well bred to enter into such accusations or revilings because they knew too well their falsehood, yet they stood by, and said nothing against them. Here is where I bring those gentlemen to the bar of justice. They listened to the abuse. They allowed it to be made use of. They profited by the political position of it, and yet said nothing; and when all is over they are simply ashamed of it — and we a.. ashamed of them.

It is not a night for such speeches; but still, as it has been my first chance to speak in public on the subject, I thought it well that you should know plainly how I felt, how proud I was of your firmness, of the calmness of your disposition. We are thought to be irritable; we are thought to be quick to return injury for injury. But they have an example, showing that when it is necessary we can be calm because we are right, we can be patient because Almighty God is patient. He knows the right must prevail. So that was. The trouble has passed over. It may come again, but if it does we should still carry out our principles, continue on as we have done, doing what is right, caring nothing for these accusations, and let the harm of it fall on the calumniators' own heads and not upon ours. Therefore, to-night, I shall drop the subject, and return you my thanks, with a full heart, for your presence here to take part in my anniversary and for the expressions of your respect and affection. My heart cannot speak all that I have felt during this day — in the church, with my clergy and people together — and to-night, with the gentlemen of the Union and their friends. The members of the Union have always had my sympathy from the beginning, and I trust that their work is only beginning. Now that this first storm has passed over, let me leave them one word of advice. They have already commenced what they call their Committee on Truth. Now is the time, not whilst people are angry, not whilst they are listening to revilings, but when all is over to give them the truth. And you, gentlemen of the Union, can do it by your words, by your example. You are mixed up in the community everywhere, in all kinds of business. When there is the time and the opportunity to put in a word for truth, do it like Christian gentlemen — not quarrelling, not in controversy, but place the truth. When there is an opportunity in the press to express to the people what is the truth, do it. Do it through your committee everywhere. Let the truth be heard, but always the truth, and not quarrelling. Thus you can carry out the object, one of the greatest objects of your Union — to express yourselves as Christian gentlemen, to give good example to others, and to help them to know that truth which you have and which is preserving you and will preserve you for all time.

As the best return I can make for your display this evening, I offer you all the affection which I have had for you in many years, and which, of course, must increase by these anniversaries. To-night I have nothing more to do, but to thank you and to say that whatever I may have done in the past I only ask of God to give me strength to do more whilst I am allowed to hold my position, and to be always worthy of this high place in which I now stand.

Long continued applause followed the close of the Archbishop's address.

The inspiring Hymn to the Pope, "Viva Leone," was then sung by the choir, and after the overture from "Wm. Tell" by the orchestra, the following Jubilee Ode, written for the occasion by Mrs. Mary E. Blake, was read by Professor Thomas A. Mullen:—

ODE.

For the Silver Jubilee of Archbishop Williams.

I.

What are the years of Time?
Pale motes that flash and fade beneath the sun;
Phantoms of grief matured and joys begun;
   Or giants striding on with steps sublime,
That echo and will echo till the last
Great trumpet tone of earthly pomp be past.
Weakest and strongest of all powers that press
The changeful souls of men to curse or bless,
   As with poor, puny skill,
They shape them to their ends for good or ill,
Making them serve as sceptre or as rod;
Foreknowing them as branches of the tree
   Of dread Eternity
That stands forever in the courts of God!

What are the years of Time?
A little span of shade, and then the light;
A little space of day and then the night;
A little spell of sorrow and delight:
   With dirges tolling or with joy bells' chime!
Swift as the winds, and aimless too as they,
Their heedless moments fleet and fly away:

Yet can their calm, slow-moving noiseless feet
Drag the great world to triumph or defeat;
Lure forceful wrong behind the prison bars,
Or lead the feeble steps of right beyond the morning stars!

II.

And the short Life of Man,
Measured by moments' span—
How shall we count its varied force, or mate
Its lordly might divine, its pitiful, poor state?
Frailer than all frail things: a flash; a breath;
A sigh expiring on the lips of death;
A reed wind-shaken; or a power supreme
Greater than height or depth; a kindling gleam
By that great light of Love Immortal thrown
Athwart the clouds by doubt or darkness driven,
To shine with ray eternal as its own,
And with Itself to share the bliss of Heaven.

III.

Time, and the Life of Man! What darkness cast
By their grim deeds doth cloud the shuddering past;
When moved alone by erring human will,
Each small ambition worked its petty ill;
Ruled its short hour with stern destroying might,
And left its pathway seared with awful blight.
Or if some kindlier impulse touched the mind
To gentler thought for welfare of mankind,
'Twas but as summer winds that come and go;
Or like the waves in motion
Above the restless ocean,
While silently the sombre depths sleep dark and cold below.

IV.

But when the Christian came, his soul aflame
With the great glory of his Master's name;

Burning with Faith, and Charity divine,
And fire of Hope that makes the world to shine
With steadfast splendor; bringing unto earth
The joy immortal of immortal birth—
Then for the first time Man, with heart elate,
Did know the worth and honor of his state.
Alone no more, nor selfishly allied
To narrow schemes of policy or pride,
To weak vain glory, to the greed of pelf,
To the poor worship of the poorer self,—
But to the Power serene that dwells above,
 Uplifted by humility of love;
Unawed by stern misfortune's fiercest blow,
Serene alike in triumph and in woe,
Made strong by sacrifice, made rich by grace,
The help, the hope, the saviour of his race.

What wondrous fire makes eloquent his speech
Whose voice inspired beyond the earth doth reach;
What strange, sweet force doth make his weakness strong,
  Whose heaven-directed hand
Is nerved by all the radiant, mighty throng
  That near the Father stand—
Fair messengers of love, who linger there
With listening hearts to hear and grace to answer prayer!

V.

Time and such Life! Ah! world that flings away
The Christian's glory from thy crown to-day,
Think, ere too late, what spendthrift fools they be
Who fling their choicest treasure in the sea;
Destroy the one sole grandeur that hath shown
To Death a greatness loftier than its own;
Kill the rich grain that future fields might bless,
And leave the world but empty nothingness.

VI.

Thou, on whose pathway to its native heaven
The silver star of Jubilee hath risen;
Thou, whose ripe years in such accord have sped
With seed of faith in virtue harvested;
Whose loving labor still hath been to raise
The spirit bowed, to joy of prayer and praise;
Whose hands upraised in benediction win
Sweet Mercy's stream to cleanse the stains of sin,—
How in thy nature's high benignant plan,
Time and the hour have blessed the life of man.

    Under thy fostering touch,
What new, fair armor hath been wove, for right
  To use against wrong's mastery, and such
Dark shapes as do with human progress fight:
  The Midas blight that turns to sordid gold
Our hopes and aspirations Eden born;
The lesser lights, that greater light do scorn;
    Doubt's haggard face and cold,
That turn to seek the gloom and shuns the face of Morn.

VII.

Prince of the House of God! what lot more blest
Than thine, that, lifted on the topmost crest
Of Faith's high mountain, the rich growth doth trace
Of thy fair realm across the centuries' space?
No passing bauble hers of mortal power;
    But for her lofty dower
Humanity's large virtues made more great;
The poor man taught to honor his estate;
Wealth made to hold its regal fee in trust,
To help the weak or hold itself accurst;
Wisdom, refined by Truth's eternal grace,
Making the world a glad abiding place
For all her children; Science seeking cause

To show the Giver greater than His laws;
And Charity, the all-ennobling gift
Which nearest to the throne of Heaven its foster-child doth lift.

VIII.

Onward her March of Empire! onward, and onward forever,
　While the spirit of life doth own its heritage proud and blest;
While misery stumbles and gropes, and joy of the earth can never
　Grant to the heart content, or give to the tortured rest.
For hers are the only gifts which man, the Immortal, prizeth;
　Hers is the light that liveth though stars and suns shall cease,
Till the stream whose fountain is God to its bountiful, source upriseth
　And the strife of the finite world is merged in infinite Peace.

MARY ELIZABETH BLAKE.

[Through the courtesy of the publisher of the *Catholic World*, we received an advance copy of Mrs. Blake's Ode, with permission to publish it in this volume.]

The exercises closed with the Te Deum, "Holy God, We Praise Thy Name," sung by the choir and the audience standing.

The audience was a notable one in every respect, and elicited unstinted praise from the visiting bishops and clergymen. It was a creditable representative gathering of the Catholics of Boston, and reflected honor on the Union and the venerated head of the archdiocese.

On the stage with the Archbishop, were Bishop De Goesbriand of Burlington, Bishop Healy of Portland, Bishop Bradley of Manchester, Bishop O'Reilly of Springfield, Bishop McQuaid of Rochester, and Bishop Conroy of Curium. The following clergymen also were present:—Very Rev. William Byrne, Very Rev. Thomas Jackson, Very Rev. Charles B. Rex, S. J.; Rev. Richard Neagle (Chancellor), Rev. Edward I. Devitt,

S. J.; Rev. James A. Doonan, S. J.; Rev. John A. Buckley, S. J.; Rev. William J. Collins, S. J.; Rev. Michael J. Hughes, S. J. Rev. Alphonsus M. Mandalari, S. J.; Rev. J. M. Schleuter. S. J.: Rev. F. X. Nopper, S. J.; Rev. J. B. Galvin, Rev. M. F. Flatley, Rev. W. J. Browne, Rev. W. D. Joyce, Rev. J. T. Remy, Rev. M. D. Murphy, Rev. D. F. Sullivan, Rev. Garrett J. Barry, Rev. Timothy Brosnahan, Rev. P. J. Daley, Rev. J. T. Dacey, Rev. G. J. Patterson, Rev. W. Fennessey, Rev. A. T. Connolly, Rev. J. E. Millerick, Rev. John J. Moore, Rev. W. H. Fitzpatrick, Rev. Robert I. Johnson, Rev. H. A. Walsh, Rev. Denis O'Callaghan, Rev. J. P. Bodfish, Rev. John A. Daley, Rev. George A. Lyons, Rev. Leo P. Boland, and Rev. P. J. Finnegan, (N.H.)

President Fitz, Hon. Thomas J. Gargan, with the Executive Committee of the Union and the Honorary Committee of ex-Presidents, also occupied seats on the stage. Mrs. M. E. Blake, the authoress of the jubilee ode, with her family, was seated on the floor, in front of the stage.

The names of the Executive Committee, the Honorary Committee, and of the Ushers will be found on page 91, with the programme as originally printed.

The following is a list of the other members of the Union, most of whom were present with their families and friends:—

William S. Pelletier.
William T. Connolly.
Samuel Tuckerman.
Bernard Foley.
Thomas J. Gargan.
Dr. John G. Blake.
Hon. P. A. Collins.
Hugh Carey.
Joseph A. Laforme.
James W. Dunphy.
Dr. J. A. McDonald.
William J. Keefe.
P. H. Powers.

William Goddard.
J. M. Prendergast.
C. A. O'Donnell.
John C. Schayer.
William H. Zinn.
James R. Murphy.
Hon. John H. O'Neil.
John A. Boyle.
Dr. P. F. Gavin.
James B. Hand.
John J. Kennedy.
Capt. J. H. Lambert.
C. E. S. MacCorry.

M. J. Ward.
Joseph Cogan.
John B. Walker.
J. Amory Sullivan.
D. B. Cashman.
John Cashman.
John E. Cassidy.
P. M. Dennon.
William Doogue.
James Dooling.
J. A. Flannagan.
John G. Ford.
Thomas Kelly.
H. F. Naphen.
Owen Nawn.
John B. O'Brien, Sheriff.
Thomas H. Devlin.
Col. John R. Farrell.
P. J. Hyde.
H. J. O'Brien.
John F. O'Brien.
Judge J. H. Burke.
C. F. Dalton.
Dr. W. A. Dunn.
J. J. McCormick.
J. M. Morrison.
James Jeffrey Roche.
Hon. Owen A. Galvin.
Jerome S. McDonald.
Nicholas M. Williams.
Dr. Michael F. Gavin.
James McCormack.
Edward Harkins.
John J. O'Donnell.
Bernard Corr.
Hon. P. H. Kendricken.
John Curtin.
John J. Mundo.

T. F. Mulrey.
Robert Bishop.
Alexander Ceppi.
Geo. W. Connor.
Thomas Sproules.
J. J. Callaghan.
M. E. Cunningham.
William E. Doyle.
C. J. Gorman.
Henry E. Lappen.
H. F. McGrady.
M. S. Morton.
Gen. M. T. Donohoe.
Henry McQuade.
J. J. Grace.
John P. Manning.
T. F. Maguire.
John Conlon.
P. F. Sullivan.
M. C. Curry.
Thomas F. Hussey.
J. S. O'Gorman.
John M. Maguire.
William P. Collins.
Dr. J. E. Dorsey.
Michael Driscoll.
Thomas Flatley.
James Keating.
John C. Kennedy.
John P. Leahy.
Joseph McHenry.
Geo. T. McLaughlin.
W. I. Pelletier.
James W. Brine.
F. G. Coughlan.
Hugh Gibben.
T. H. Cummings.
A. W. Doyle.

P. J. Flatley.
Thomas Riley.
David A. Ring.
P. Ambrose Dowd.
Bernard McCann.
Francis Groll.
J. P. Kennedy.
J. B. McAloon.
Thomas O. Callahan.
Jas. W. O'Brien.
Henry O'Meara.
Wm. Peard.
J. Manley Pieper.
Aug. D. Small.
Dr. J. M. Thompson.
John H. Brine.
John A. Devlin.
John B. Donovan.
Thos. F. Galvin.
Dr. T. J. Giblin.
Patrick Howe.
Geo. McCarthy.
D. A. Noonan.
James F. Powers.
M. H. Quigley.
D. W. Shea.
Dr. P. J. Timmins.
Thomas M. Watson.
Thomas A. Whalen.
M. L. Madden.
Chas. A. Smith.
Chas. J. Countie.
Edw. W. Clive.
D. C. Dillworth.
Thomas Gaffney.
Joseph F. Hearn.
F. L. Maguire.
Clarence H. Pike.

Hon. E. J. Flynn.
Dr. W. H. Grainger.
T. F. Haley.
William H. Hardy.
William P. Henry.
James J. Herrick.
T. J. Lane.
Thomas A. Mullen.
Sig. A. Rotoli.
Geo. H. Salloway.
Edw. J. Shaughness.
James A. Gallivan.
Eugene F. Donnelly.
Andrew W. Bligh.
Geo. F. Robey.
Henry Dobbins.
Peter P. Corbett.
T. H. Keenan.
Edward Murphy.
John J. Haley.
James F. Sweeney.
John W. O'Mealy.
Michael J. Dwyer.
James P. Bevins.
Wm. Sullivan.
Jas. L. Gethins.
Jos. A. Ryan.
Dr. M. W. O'Keefe.
G. T. J. Culhane.
Thomas McLaughlin.
Neil McNeill.
D. W. Mahoney.
H. B. McMahon.
Fred J. Crosby.
Thos J. McMahon.
Geo. W. Smith.
Daniel Clark.
T. H. Hanley.

Francis J. Weller.
Dr. Thos. J. Ball.
J. B. Whelton.
Chas. E. McLaughlin
John H. Corcoran.
John B. Finn.
W. J. Lally.
John J. Dowling.
Dr. J. P. Lumbard.
Edw. A. Paige.
John J. Madden.
Stephen A. Casey.
P. Frank Tracy.
Eugene E. Devlin.
Geo. C. Corcoran.
Frank K. Browne.
Joseph T. Mooney.
John F. Muldoon.
Wm. J. Dolan.
Francis X. Corr.
Dr. F. J. Keliher.
Wm. H. Lynch.
Dr. D. M. McIntyre.
C. B. McCormick.
V. H. Ober.
Dr. C. W. McDonald.
George D'Arcy.
Manasses P. Morgan.
J. J. Donnelly.

Dr. H. C. Towle.
James N. Friel.
Jos. A. Campbell.
N. W. Thornton.
A. V. Norton.
T. W. Norton.
Peter T. Connor.
John H. Casey.
Dominick Toy.
Jos. M. Kiggen.
C. I. Quirk.
John A Brett.
Dr. Hilary Tucker Sweeney.
James C. Bertie.
S. A Keeler.
W. L. Mooney.
P. J. Kane.
Wm. H. Howe.
R. S. Carven.
D. W. O'Brien.
M. W. Phalan.
Jos. F. Carew.
W. C. O'Leary.
Michael Fitzpatrick.
John J. Bligh.
Frank Dowling.
John E. Lappen.
E. J. Machugh.

The music was finely rendered and gave general satisfaction. The bouquet of artists comprised the best soloists from the Catholic church choirs in Boston, and the orchestra under the direction of Mr. John C. Mullaly was selected from the best symphony musicians in the city.

The programme as originally printed is given on pages 91 to 94.

SILVER JUBILEE CELEBRATIONS

IN HONOR OF THE CONSECRATION OF

MOST REV. JOHN J. WILLIAMS, D. D.

BY

ST. JAMES PARISHIONERS,

NOTRE DAME ACADEMY,

AND

SACRED HEART ACADEMY.

ADDRESS AND PRESENTATION

FROM

PARISHIONERS OF ST. JAMES.

At the episcopal residence on Union Park street, Tuesday evening, March 10, the Most Rev. Archbishop was pleased to receive a committee of ladies and gentlemen from St. James' parish, bearing a congratulatory address and a magnificent souvenir of silver and quartered oak. The committee was composed as follows:—

William H. Dowling (chairman), John J. McDonald (secretary), Rev. William P. McQuaid (pastor), John A. Duggan, Daniel F. Sullivan, David J. Gleason, Mrs. John A. Duggan, Miss M. Ryan, Mrs. Mary Flannigan, Michael T. Callahan, Thomas Power, John Lyons, John Sullivan, Charles E. Colbert, John Quinn.

The address, which was written by Mr. Dowling, was artistically engrossed on parchment, mounted on heavy card stock and bound on bishop's purple morocco. The following is a copy of the address:—

Your Grace — It is with more than mere formality that we, as representatives of St. James' parish, congratulate you on this the silver judlee of your consecration as bishop.

With one acclaim the 500,000 Catholics in the archdiocese of Boston rejoice today that the providence of God sent to preside over this particular flock one who has had such a singular successful career.

Some will point with pride to the saintly character of your life as a model for your clergy and your people, and to the perfect justice with which you administered the affairs of your high office. Others will dwell on the condition of the church at the time of your consecration, the marvellous increase in its numbers, and in the prosperity of your people. When the eloquence of speech fails to properly express the wonderful business sagacity that will always be associated with your fame, the Holy Cross Cathedral, the many churches, convents, schools, colleges, hospitals, charitable institutions, and the St. John's Seminary, will be pointed to as having multiplied so rapidly that they seem to have been erected as if by the magic of your touch.

While uniting with the members of all congregations in the archdiocese, yet the members of St. James' parish have especial cause for rejoicing. It was Rev. John J. Williams who in 1849 collected the children who lived within what are now the limits of St. James' parish and organized a Sunday School in a hall on Albany street. It was in the Sunday School hall (which was later transferred to Beach street, and became known as the Chapel of the Holy Family) that Father Williams called a meeting of the people who lived in that district and proposed to them the necessity of erecting a church, which proposition was adopted and the work undertaken at once. It was Very Rev. John J. Williams, Vicar-General, who rescued St. James' church from impending financial difficulties when he was appointed its pastor in 1857. It was Very Rev. Father Williams who administered the parochial affairs of the parish for nine years, and by his zeal and devotion, in guarding the spiritual and material welfare of his flock, won their everlasting gratitude and love. It was in old St. James' church on Albany street that Very Rev. John J. Williams was consecrated Rt. Rev. John J. Williams and bishop of Boston.

Thus, Your Grace, St. James' congregation has especial reason to be proud of your most successful episcopate, and in order to give some tangible evidence which may serve to recall your pastorate with St. James' church, as well as the deep interest which the entire congregation has taken in the celebration of your silver jubilee, we present you with this souvenir.

We pray God, who has blessed your people with such a long period of happiness and prosperity, that He may spare you as their shepherd for many years to come, and that each succeeding anniversary of this event will be but a prelude to the outburst of increased love and veneration that will greet you on the celebration of the golden jubilee of your priesthood.

The Archbishop responded in a few well chosen words, expressing his thanks for the beautiful souvenir and for the kind words in the address He evidently was deeply touched by this tribute of respect from his old parish of St. James.

The souvenir which was presented is of beautiful design and workmanship, and will form a pleasant reminder of a very noteworthy occasion. The centre piece is of solid silver, with elegantly chased borders, and at each of the corners bears a representation of the scenes of the Archbishop's labors at various stages of his life.

At the left-hand upper corner is a representation of the old Cathedral on Franklin street, and at the lower left-hand corner is represented old St. James' church. The upper right-hand corner contains an engraving of the new Cathedral, and the lower corner on the same side one of the new St. James' church on Harrison avenue. On the left is the date 1866, and on the right 1891.

The centrepiece bears the inscription: — " Souvenir of the Silver Jubilee of the Most Rev. John Joseph Williams, Archbishop of Boston, March 11, 1891. Presented by the Parish of St. James, Boston."

Immediately over this plate is the seal of the archdiocese. Over that again is the monogram of the Archbishop, "J. J. W.," and surmounting all are the emblems of His Grace's exalted office, the mitre and crozier.

In raised letters close to the edge is the inscription "Sacerdos in æternum, ad multos annos."

The silver plate is set into a frame of richly carved oak, replete with religious designs, the whole being about three feet by two, and is intended to rest on an easel, also specially designed.

RECEPTION

BY THE

PUPILS OF NOTRE DAME

OF THE

ARCHDIOCESE OF BOSTON.

Perhaps the most interesting and significant of the receptions tendered to the Most Reverend Archbishop by the lambs of his flock was that at the Academy of Notre Dame, Berkeley Street, Boston, on Tuesday, March 10. Here the delegates from thirty parochial schools — representing 11,500 pupils — and the Superioresses of the twenty houses of Notre Dame in Massachusetts, rose to greet His Grace as he entered the hall with the following clergymen: Mgr. Griffin, Rev. T. J. Conaty, Worcester; Rev. Wm. H. Duncan, S. J., Rev. M. F. Byrne, S. J., Rev. B. F. Killilea, Rev. Wm. P. McQuaid, Rev. James J. O'Brien, Rev. J. J. Nilan, Rev. P. Billings, Rev. Richard J. Barry, Rev. F. X. Nopper, S.J., Rev. E. J. Devitt, S. J., Rev. Richard Neagle, chancellor of the archdiocese, Rev. H. A. Sullivan, Rev. Denis O'Callaghan, Rev. Thomas Shahan, Arlington; Rev. Thomas Scully, Cambridgeport; Rev. J. W. McMahon, Rev. C. J. McGrath, Somerville; Rev. James T. O'Reilly, O. S. A., Lawrence; Rev. Timothy Brosnahan, Waltham; Rev. M. F. Murphy, Hopkinton; and Rev. H. R. O'Donnell, East Boston. The editor of the Pilot, Mr. Patrick Donahoe, was also present.

The exhibition hall, where the reception was held, was decorated as befitted the joyful occasion. Stately palms filled the recesses of the windows and were grouped about the dais, speaking of the victories of the champion of the Lord; bright-hued flowers told of the children's love and clinging vines of their filial dependence on the good shepherd, the father and guardian of thousands of souls; but more eloquent than all were the bright faces, the beaming eyes, of the children themselves, who had earned by hard work for many months the right to be present, for the delegates chosen were the two pupils in the tenth grade of each school who had received the highest percentage at the last examinations. It was the fairest way of selecting one for an honor coveted by all.

Below we print the programme. It speaks well for the uniform excellence of the training in the schools of Notre Dame that the numbers passed off as smoothly as though all the details of preparation had been the labor of one teacher, whereas the performers had met but twice before the eventful day. It was worthy of the honored guest to select the best talent, without regard to the location of the schools.

PROGRAMME.

March . . . . Fenimore.
   Pianos: Misses Walter, Hagerty, Madden and
       McQuaid.
 Organ: Miss English.
 Guitar: Misses Dore, Mahoney, Guilmette, Timmins and
      Corbett.
 Bells: Misses Yates and McDonald. Berkeley Street.
Salutatory . . . .
 Written by Miss Barry. Spoken by Miss Lane.
          Berkeley Street.
Hail to our Prelate. Chorus . . . . Mendelssohn.

A DIAMOND SET IN SILVER.

PROLOGUE AND PART I.

Many are calleD; but Chosen few.
One heard that voiCe: "Come, follow Me."
Rose and followed Him eXuLting.
Master, I will liVe for Thee.
Written by Miss Dodd. Spoken by Miss Canty. Boston.

Polonaise brilliante . . . . Weber.
  Misses McSweeney, E. and M. Murphy and McCarty. Lowell.
Ave Maria. Vocal quartet . . . . Abt.
  Misses White, Milard, Drummond and Clark. Roxbury.

PART II.

Many a Day of ConfliCt
The holy Cross will see,
Naught is so sure as battLe,
EXcept the VIctory.

        Miss Joyce. Lowell.

An old time strain.
 Harp, Miss McNulty. Piano, Miss Matson. Roxbury.

PART III.

A Man we honor now with louD aCClaim,
Yet know his deeds ConceaLed from eye of fame
EXcel the eXcellence we striVe to name.

        Miss Kenny. Roxbury.

O Quam Suavis . . . . Cagliero.
  Misses N. and E. Murphy and Guillmette. Lowell.

PART IV.

May Days without a Cloud suCCeed; we pray,
The joy eXCeeding great of this brIght day.

Written by Miss Doherty. Spoken by Miss Devine, Berkeley Street.

Norma Duo, ... Rosellen.
  Misses Hughes and Morse.
Te Deum, full chorus . . . . Berkeley Street.

The programme, printed in silver and royal purple, a pretty little specimen of the typographical art, bore on one page the following thoughtful sonnet, commemorating the fact that the name of "the disciple whom Jesus loved" belongs to three of the four great men who have filled the See of Boston, and has been given to the life-work of Archbishop Williams, St. John's Theological Seminary Brighton.

BOSTON, MARCH 11, 1891.

> Saint Botolph's Town! Far over leagues of land
> And leagues of sea looks forth its noble tower,
> And far around the chiming bells are heard.
> *Longfellow, Boston.*

Nay, not Saint Botolph's, but Saint John's Town! Thou
  Hast borne so long his favor, let him claim
  For this one happy day his meed of fame,
While we recount the memories that endow
The century that closes round us now
  Since the great Cheverus to thy portals came,
  Whose Christ-like charity, untouched of blame,
Hearts cold and erring made in homage bow.
Fitzpatrick, — in such "times as tried men's souls,"—
  Soldier and saint, the mitre grandly wore,
And, dying, left the spirit that controls
  His life and Cheverus', to a third who bore
Saint John's dear name, and on the living scrolls
  Of priestly hearts writes it forever more.

The salutatory, which was written by Miss Barry, was delivered in a most graceful manner by Miss Lane. Both young ladies are pupils of the academy at Berkeley street.

SALUTATORY.

Welcome as the breath of springtime
  When the winter's chill is past,
When through meads the blooming flowers,
  Breaking forth, now smile at last.

Or, as e'en the softened flush that
  Tints the dawn with purple ray
Is your presence, honored prelate,
  In our happy midst to-day.

Oh, may these bright, fleeting moments
  Be for you as swift they fly,
Sweet as are the honeyed perfumes
  In the hyacinths that lie.

Fitting 'tis that we who bear the
    Loved, endearing title true,
Of Our Lady's chosen children,
    Should now prove our love for you.

Who the client constant, faithful are
    Of John, whom Christ loved best,
To whose care on Calvary's summit
    He resigned His mother blest.

Let the muse by bards be courted,
    Who her fame-lit heights explore
As on pinions bright of thought
    To fancy's realm they proudly soar.

Not the glowing flame we envy,
    Kindled in the poet's breast;
Happier far is our blessed portion
    Thus to greet our honored guest.

Ah! enough for us this day
    At love's fair shrine to sweetly bend,
And the shepherd of the sheep to greet
    As father, guardian, friend.

Loved Archbishop, honored prelate,
    Pastors kind, to you all,
We extend a cordial welcome
    Now within this convent hall.

As unto the vase long broken
    Clings the fragrance of the flowers,
Such will be the recollections
    Of those joyous, happy hours.

Till long years shall all have vanished,
    And we greet with joy untold,
Not the jubilee of silver,
    But the brighter one of gold.

"A Diamond Set in Silver" was the title chosen by one of the graduates for the complimentary poem, written by four young ladies, and she thus ingeniously explains it in the

PROLOGUE.

I.

Our title? Is there need I should explain?
  They cut a diamond with many sides,
  And each of these the ray of light divides,
  And all of them the rainbow hues retain,
  Which, flashing back, a greater lustre gain.
    Now, I compare a soul wherein resides
    The sunlight of God's grace whate'er betides
To such a gem, nor, can I think, in vain.
So, as we look on this exalted life,
  In all its phases,— student, youth or priest,
  Bishop, archbishop, at the Master's call,—
View it in paths of peace, or fields of strife.
  And every year its brilliancy increased,
  Say, was it not a diamond through it all?

II.

In flashing gems the ray of light is broke,
  The splendor to our vision is a screen.
  And which of us could draw the line between
A young Eulalia, rushing to the stroke,
  And meek Aquinas, with his heart of oak,
Or sweet St. Agnes, martyred at thirteen,
And Chrysostom, who sixty years had seen,
  Or Paul, from whose white locks a century spoke!
Poets may love to paint the young and fair,
  And we to think mere children were so brave;
    But what might tell the Book of Life alone
With decade or with century written there,
  God knows, Who unto each His graces gave.
    The years are but the setting of the stone.

III.

And yet "Fine pictures suit in frames as fine,"
Old Thomas Tusser said, and so say we,
"Consistency's a jewel," added he.
Yes, though the soul, that diamond divine,
Can find ,no setting it doth not outshine.
  So, honored prelate, we have prayed for thee,
  (To borrow phrases from our greeting glee)
Long years thy life may with our own entwine,
Archbishops, like the Popes, "are of no age;"
  Live then till God, who knows the secret sought
  So fruitlessly by alchemists of old
And told alone to Father Time the sage,
  In workshops of the centuries shall have wrought
  The Diamond's silver setting into gold.

The chronograms on the programme mark the years of the Archbishop's ordination, 1845; of his consecration, 1866; of his investiture with the pallium, 1875; and of his twenty-fifth anniversary, 1891.

In reply the Archbishop said :—

"My dear children, I thank you for all your good wishes for the future and for all the beautiful words said of the past. The language you have used speaks well for the training and education you have received; still I must acknowledge that had your encomiums been uttered of another it would have been less embarassing for me to have listened. When a man, however, makes up his mind to live twenty-five years a bishop, he must pay the penalty. It is certainly a great pleasure to see before me the representatives of so many schools, bearing the impress of the same training.

"Among the many works you have attributed to me there is one you could not mention, and that is the introduction of your devoted teachers into the diocese. It is not my honor to have brought them, but my consolation to possess them, for they are the glory of the diocese. There are other teaching orders who do their work, and do it well, but the Sisters of Notre Dame came first.

"When you return to your respective schools bear my blessing to your companions and to your teachers, and thank them for the great work they are doing in the diocese,"

The pupils presented an exquisitely illuminated address, the work of one of the Sisters. It is painted on French beveled glass, measuring thirty-six by twenty-nine inches, the design being Easter lillies, ferns and palms, in lustrous green and mother of pearl tints, and the lettering a rich purple on a silver ground. Slender scrolls winding in and out, furnish places for the names of the schools and the number of pupils in each. It is framed in silver and lavender plush. The twenty-three lines of this address epitomize the feelings of New England Catholics and of Catholic Bostonians wherever they may have wandered from the Hub, though they are headed

NOTRE DAME'S TRIBUTE TO OUR BELOVED ARCHBISHOP.

Come higher, Friend — Feed thou my lambs, my sheep,
   The Master's words, the poetry of Heaven,
      On this glad day should prelude every song.
Now five and twenty years His flocks you keep
   Where rivers flow through pastures green along,
      Though your own path o'er thorny ways has striven.
Shepherd of souls! Your sheep God's levites are,
   Your lambs, His people trusted to their care,
Who pray from full hearts' fervor when Life's Star,
   The Chalice they uplift in morning air,
And speak the names which Jesus loves to hear,
   For thoughts of that Last Supper, when a John
Leaned on His Heart, remembering Nazareth dear
   When Joseph toiled for Mary and her Son.
Ah! then we pray all blessings may come down
   On you, who from the great Fitzpatrick's hand

Took Cheverus' staff and Fenwick's, which you hold
So worthily the flower of its renown
The years touch not to wither, but expand.
When, dearest Lord, ten thousand thousand pray,
"May he, the Angel of Saint Botolph's Town,
Remain with us till silver years are gold,"
Say, as of John, "So will I have him stay."

GRADUATE OF NOTRE DAME.

GIFT OF THE SISTERS OF NOTRE DAME.

The gift of the Sisters of Notre Dame to the Most Reverend Archbishop for his silver jubilee was a painted dinner-set of nearly two hundred pieces. It is the work of four Sisters, the teachers of painting at Roxbury and Berkeley street and the Novitiate Training School, Waltham; and kept their clever heads and fingers busy for two months. As a work of art, it is exquisite; as a souvenir, unique. Here are painted all the buildings connected with the Archbishop's life: the church of his baptism; St. Sulpice, where he was ordained priest; St. James, the scene of his pastoral labors and of his consecration; the old Cathedral, hallowed by a thousand tender memories of the saintly "Bishop John"; the new Cathedral, his legacy of labor to his young coadjutor, where the latter received the pallium; the episcopal residence; and finally, St. John's Seminary, Brighton, and the new Philosophy Hall, the crowning work of these twenty-five busy years. These grace the large platters, but places are found elsewhere for every conceivable twist and turn of an artistic hand in water-lilies, blush roses, pansies, ferns, and the old-fashioned sweet-williams in all their colors, the latter being in some variety on every piece, as well as the Archbishop's coat-of-arms, all on a straw-colored ground with silver and gold filigree. The fish-set is ornamented with pictures of the shy beauties of brook and stream, on a sea-green ground. The game-set pays the same tribute to the shyer denizens of the woods, on a ground color borrowed from the fawn. Nor are landscapes forgotten, there being twelve scenes of lovely hill and vale. There are views also of the convents of Notre Dame, Roxbury, Berkeley street, and Walnut Hills, Cincinnati. The dinner-plates are ornamented with a spray of sweet-williams enclosing a space (the shape varying with every plate) whereon is printed in gilt one of the following little poems, or one of the chronograms elsewhere noted:

> Because thy birthplace and the home
> Of all thy life and linked with all
> Sacred and tender memories,
> The city given thee by Rome,
> Oh! suffer the past she should recall.
> Not less her own thy glory is.

> Joy, love and gratitude sincere
> Join in the wish that one so dear
> Will live to see the Golden Year.

> "Hail to the chief who in triumph advances!"
>   Little the bard knew of chief such as ou s,
> Victor of souls, whose kind heat enhances
>   The courage that dares, the rank that empowers.

> "In hoc vinces." Cross, thou alone hast seen
> All tempests rise, and leave thee yet serene.

> Oh! Singer but so lately passed away,
> We miss the strength and sweetness of the lay
> Your heart, O'Reilly, would have sung to-day.

> "Rien qu'un évêque, mais tout cela,"
> Glory of France the speaker was. And we
> Have seen at home how grand that "*all*" may be.

The noblest work where all
  Is nobly done,
'Twere hard to name, and yet
  We think of one—
His loved St. John's, which bears
  The future's hope —
Not earth, but Heaven alone
  Can tell its scope.

"See the conquering hero comes,"
Not mid the blare of Trumpets, roll of drums,
But like his meek and humble Master wearing
The Shepherd's fleece, the Holy Cross upbearing.

It happened that there were two spaces on the plate bearing the reference to John Boyle O'Reilly, so long associated with the Most Reverend Archbishop on the *Pilot*. The artist very appropriately filled the smaller one with a view of Bunker Hill Monument, under whose shadow this "truest of all the true" lovers of liberty spent the happiest years of his well-earned life of freedom and wrote those stirring lyrics that but make us feel more keenly his silence while his beloved Boston sings her Vivat to the "Veteran of the jubilee." But God's will be done, even though our

  "Lycidas is dead before his prime,
  And he has not left a peer."

GRADUATE OF NOTRE DAME.

HISTORICAL.

May the writer of the above add an item of the Catholic history of Boston which has been overlooked by the historians, although unconsciously? In the "garden enclosed" of the convent of Notre Dame, Berkeley street, took place the first procession of the Blessed Sacrament, in the open air, ever seen in Boston. It was on the feast of the Sacred Heart of

Jesus, 1865, which that year fell on the twenty-fifth of June. Rev. Fr. Buteaux, a venerable old French priest who was convent chaplain at that time, obtained a rather reluctant consent from Bishop Fitzpatrick, who feared the hour had not yet come for open-air demonstrations of Catholicity. Everything passed off very quietly, however, and the permission was cordially given for the following years. Many of those who walked in that first procession live yet and tell the younger generation of its beauty and the devotion it excited in all hearts. Benediction of the Blessed Sacrament was given at an altar erected in the garden, and again on re-entering the chapel.

The Back Bay was then a waste of sand, over which the tide wandered at will. Trinity Church, the Art Museum, the palatial Vendome, Brunswick, and Berkeley, Commonwealth Avenue and the grand residences of Bostonians possessed of wealth very uncommon, — all these were unknown and many of them undreamed of. The Institute of Technology was the convent's nearest neighbor. When a very few years — less than a decade — had seen the desert reclaimed and houses springing up everywhere, the processions in the open air were abandoned, at first for prudential reasons, and later because taking place at most of the churches. The memory of those practical acts of faith in the Real Presence remains very dear, however, and that the children of the future may not lose sight of this glory of the past, a shrine to the Sacred Heart has been erected on the terrace of the garden, bearing this legend on the front of the modest altar :—

This Shrine commemorates
the Feast of the Sacred Heart of Jesus, June 25, 1865,
when, by permission of Rt. Rev. J. B. Fitzpatrick,
the Blessed Sacrament
was borne in solemn procession through the garden;
it being the first time such a ceremony took
place in open air since the foundation of Boston.

RECEPTION

AT THE

ACADEMY OF THE SACRED HEART.

The silver jubilee of the Most Rev. Archbishop was honored in an appropriate manner by the pupils of the Academy of the Sacred Heart, Chester Park, on the morning of March 16th. The study hall was beautifully decorated for the grand occasion. A throne was made for His Grace, and surrounding it were baskets and bouquets of choice flowers.

The programme was very interesting and showed the high plane of excellence the pupils had attained. The welcome chorus by all the pupils on the entrance of the archbishop and clergy was extremely fine.

The next number was a French dialogue between the Misses M. Kenney, Agnes Moran, Maria Raymon, Katie Murray, Marie Eagan, May Loyd, Katie McGlynn, delivered with such proficiency in the language as to make one imagine they were real Parisians.

The Largo-Handel violin, piano, and organ executed by the Misses M. Latero, piano; Mary Masterson, organ; and Loretto O'Callaghan, violin; was perfect, and called forth much admiration.

"St. Ignatius," by Miss Louise O'Brien of Charlestown, was beautifully rendered. A vocal trio costa, by the Misses A. Rooney, A. Field and F. Freeman, was followed by an address, delivered by Miss Mary Curtin.

At the close of the exercises the pupils tendered His Grace an immense basket of jacqueminot roses, bordered with silver greetings. Other floral tributes were tendered him, forming a floral hedge around the distinguished guest.

The Archbishop made a brief but eloquent address, after which he gave his blessing. With him was the Very Rev. William Byrne, V. G., Rev. Dr. Talbot, Rev. R. Neagle, chancellor, Rev. Father Boland, Rev. Father Walsh, Rev. Father Sullivan, Rev. Father

O'Toole, Rev. Father Doonan, S. J.; Rev. Father Devitt, S. J.; Rev. Father McGurck, S. J.; and Rev. Father Hendrick of Rochester, New York.

EXTRAORDINARY GENERAL MEETING

OF THE

SOCIETY OF ST. VINCENT DE PAUL.

CONGRATULATORY ADDRESS

By the President for the Society,

Addresses by other Gentlemen,

AND THE

ARCHBISHOP'S REPLY.

EXTRAORDINARY GENERAL MEETING

OF THE

SOCIETY OF ST. VINCENT DE PAUL,

SUNDAY, APRIL 5, 1891.

The "extraordinary general meeting" of the Society of St. Vincent de Paul on Sunday evening, April 5, 1891, in the basement chapel of the Cathedral, in honor of the silver jubilee of the Most Rev. Archbishop, was the most interesting meeting ever held by the Society. The details were arranged by President Thomas F. Ring and Secretary John J. Mundo, and carried out satisfactorily with the assistance of members of Holy Cross Conference. Every Conference in Boston and vicinity was well represented, and many had every member present. At eight o'clock, when the Archbishop appeared, accompanied by Very Rev. Wm. Byrne, V. G., Rev. Leo P. Boland, Rev. R. Neagle, Rev. Fathers Sullivan and Talbot, and President Ring, the chapel was well filled by the members and their friends. Occupying seats in front were Rev. John O'Brien of East Cambridge; Rev. J. A. Buckley, S. J.; Rev. J. P. M. Schleuter, S. J., Holy Trinity; Rev. Joseph F. Mohan, Everett; Mr Patrick Donahoe, editor of the *Pilot;* Mr. John Conlon, and Mr. M. A. Ring of New York.

After the opening prayer by the Spiritual Director of the Particular Council, Very Rev. Wm. Byrne, V. G., and spiritual reading by Vice-President Shay, a summary of the Conference report for the quarter ending March 31, was read by Secretary Mundo. Superintendent Keefe then made a brief report of the Special Work for the care of destitute and abandoned children.

The second part of the exercises was opened by the President calling upon Mr. James Collins, first President of the Particular Council, who was invited to be present, but was unavoidably absent.

Dr. Thomas Dwight, President of Holy Cross Conference, was next called. He began by saying that on meeting to celebrate the Silver Jubilee of His Grace members naturally spoke of his connection with the Society of St. Vincent de Paul. They wished to thank him for having founded it in Boston, and the better to appreciate the value of this gift it was fitting to consider what might be called the characteristic note of the Society. This note is that it is a Catholic benevolent society. There are many other societies in the community to help the poor, to distribute help, to keep records, to send visitors, to teach trades to children; all these are good, but in themselves philanthropic. Putting aside all revelation and religion, it is hard to see any reason for loving one's neighbor, but christianity shows us why. We should love our neighbor because of the command of our Divine Master. We should love him because he has been created for a glorious eternity such as it has not entered into the heart of man to conceive. These are supernatural reasons, and they are the ones that animated the founders of the society and must animate those who would be worthy of them. From this point of view it is impossible for us to patronize the poor man. We go to him as friend to friend, knowing that whatever good we may do him, we do far more to ourselves. The speaker then referred to the fact that the members were becoming too old, and that young men should be welcomed and encouraged. He ended by hoping that His Grace might long be spared to watch the growth of the society.

Mr. Thos. B. Fitz, President of the Catholic Union, was the next speaker. He congratutated the society on its great work, and said the speaking should be left to the members of the Conferences, who are entitled to all the credit. To him the pleasantest feature was to see so many of the sons following in the footsteps of their fathers, preparing to take up the work and continue it in the true spirit of christian charity. Every act should have a supernatural motive, doing good because it pleases God. The most eloquent speeches to-night were the report of the Secretary, giving facts and figures, and that of Mr. Keefe, showing the number of neglected children cared for by the society.

Mr. John W. Keily, President of the Paticular Council of Providence, R. I., was then called upon. He said he was pleased to be present to pay a tribute of respect to the Most Rev. Archbishop, and to thank him for establishing the society in the East. The good work was being carried on in Providence under the spiritual administration of a prelate after the Archbishop's own heart, whose fruitful deeds show that the seeds sown in Boston were carefully planted. Let us endeavor to carry out the spirit of the society's rules, and gain for the poor and ourselves all its spiritual favors.

Mr. Thomas F. Ring, as President of the Central and Particular Councils, then presented the following address for the whole society:—

MOST REVEREND ARCHBISHOP—

The Society of St. Vincent de Paul as represented by the Conferences attached to the Particular Council of Boston, desires to pay its tribute of honor and respect and to join in the congratulations and good wishes that come to you from clergy and laity on the occasion of your silver jubilee. While as faithful Catholics we heartily share in all the expressions of affection that the twenty-fifth anniversary of your consecration as bishop of Boston brings forth, we remember it was your hand that in St. James' parish planted the first Conference in the diocese, and whatever of good to the poor, spiritually and materially, has followed as a consequence of the growth of the society, is largely due to you, who watched with a fatherly care over its first days here, and who has been its friend and constant benefactor since.

Our offering to your jubilee is the record of the poor, the sick, the orphans and neglected children, who have been assisted by the society you established in this city.

It will not be the least of the happy incidents of this day, to know that the seed sown by you has brought forth abundant fruit; that measured by the standard of money, more than half a million of dollars has gone to feed and shelter the poor through the channel your charity opened when you organized the first Conference in Boston.

Our Conferences, therefore, feel it is proper they should reverentially salute you as their father in works of charity, and to beg Almighty God, the father of the poor, to bless you and to long spare you to clergy and people, the head of the archdiocese of Boston.

[Signed]

FOR THE PARTICULAR COUNCIL.

WILLIAM BYRNE, V. G., Spiritual Director.
THOMAS F. RING, President.
J. J. KENNEDY, Vice-President.
THOMAS SHAY, Vice-President.
JOHN J. MUNDO, Secretary.
J. W. McDONALD, Treasurer.

FOR THE CONFERENCES.

DANIEL F. SULLIVAN, President St. James.
THOMAS DWIGHT, President Holy Cross.
DENNIS J. COLLINS, President SS. Peter and Paul.
MICHAEL CARNEY, President St. Mary.
JOSEPH S. O'GORMAN, President Immaculate Conception.
THOMAS J. GIBLIN, President Gate of Heaven.
THOMAS J. LANE, President Holy Redeemer.
PATRICK J. GREEN, President St. Stephen.
WALTER J. O'MALLEY, President St. Patrick.
JOHN B. FITZPATRICK, President St. Joseph.
PATRICK DOODY, President St. Augustine.
MICHAEL LOWRY, President St. Mary, Cambridge.
JOHN A. MAGUIRE, President St. Rose.
DANIEL B. SHAUGHNESSY, President St. John.
JOHN O'BRIEN, President Sacred Heart.
JOHN A. FINNEGAN, President St. Mary, Charlestown.
JOHN H. KELLY, President St. Joseph, Circuit Street.
M. J. CONNELLY, Pres. St. Francis de Sales, B. Highlands.
JOHN McSORELY, President St. Mary, Everett.
DENIS FOLEY, President St. Paul.

JOHN H. CRONIN, President St. Thomas.
JOHN CONWAY, President St. Francis De Sales, Charlestown.
C. J. McCORMICK, President St. Mary, Waltham.
CHARLES E. McCARTY, President St. Joseph, Somerville.
WILLIAM J. SLOAN, President St. Peter, Dorchester.
JAMES B. HAND, President St. Mary, Brookline.
JOHN S. SHERIDAN, President St. Peter, Cambridge.
PATRICK T. HANLEY, President Our Lady of Perpetual Help.
A. A. BURGOYNE, President Assumption.
DAVID F. LONG, President St. Catherine.
ROBERT L. WHITE, President St. Peter Claver.
RICHARD H. FARLEY, President St. Columbkille.
MATTHIAS BROCK, President Holy Trinity.
EDWARD J. BURKE, President Aspirant Conference.
RICHARD KEEFE, Agent Special Work.

Mr. Thomas Power, an original member of the St. James Conference, and an old friend of the Archbishop, was then called upon. After some urging he stood up and said it was thirty-one years since the first Conference was established in St. James parish. "On the invitation of our pastor, the present Archbishop, ten men got together in my house. All ten are gone now, except the Archbishop and myself. I know that the Archbishop is fond of short speeches, and I shall not make this one any longer."

Mr. Matthias Brock, President of Holy Trinity Conference (German), made the following remarks, first in German and afterwards in English :—

Most Reverend Archbishop —

May it please Your Grace to receive in behalf of the Holy Trinity Conference of St. Vincent de Paul, connected with the German Church of this city, the hearty congratulations upon the twenty-fifth anniversary of your consecration as bishop of Boston. It is useless for me to attempt to improve upon the words spoken in praise of the colossal labor performed by you in the interest of our holy religion during the past twenty-five years. Hosts of organizations have met to do you honor on this occasion; none, however, can excel in fervor the hearty good wishes tendered to you this evening by the Brothers of St. Vincent de Paul. In Your Grace we find a living example of all that is noble in the true man of God. We have seen the great growth of the diocese under your energetic administration; everywhere churches, chapels, schools and asylums have been reared to meet the increasing wants of the faithful. Surely the blessing of Almighty God is with you in your undertakings.

As members of the various Conferences we are trying to emulate you in that christian example, as reflected in your noble career. We have reason to know that you approve our organization. This should be sufficient to spur onward every member of our brotherhood to seek and provide means for the comfort of the poor and infirm. While this is surely a noble work, one equally as noble, thanks to that Catholic spirit of the officers of the Central Council, who have seen the necessity and hence provided means for saving neglected and homeless children. To appreciate all that has been done in this direction, it is only necessary to read the report of our Special Agent. To accomplish such special work as this, caused our Spiritual Director to call a small number of men together for the purpose of instituting a Conference in our parish. Experience of only a few months has shown us that this is a fruitful field to work in. What can be more elevating than to provide for the children of unfortunate parents, to see that they are brought to their church and school, in order that they may be taught the rudiments of our holy Catholic religion. In this special labor, Most Reverend Archbishop, the Holy Trinity Conference unites with all other Conferences to ask your special blessing.

Mr. Robert L. White, President St. Peter Claver Conference (colored men's), spoke as follows:—

My Lord and Most Venerable Archbishop, it is with grateful hearts we assemble here to-night as a part of the militant Holy Mother Church to give God thanks for the many graces

He has bestowed upon you, and for that still greater grace, the inspiration of the Holy Ghost to establish a society in your diocese bearing the name of St. Vincent de Paul, the great apostle of charity. The humble Conference of St. Peter Claver assemble, composed of the Sons of Ethiopia, to return thanks for the many graces bestowed upon you, hoping that the day is not far off when those venerable ears of yours will listen to the Sons of Ethiopia chanting the hallelujah in your diocese, praises to God! Then it might be said, with holy Simeon, "Dismiss thy servant, O Lord, for my eyes have beheld the days of thy salvation."

Master Edward J. Burke, President Aspirant Conference Immaculate Conception, spoke for the boys in an appropriate manner.

After the delivery of the addresses, His Grace responded substantially as follows :—

Mr. President and Gentlemen: — It is scarcely necessary for me to say how much pleasure it is to me to receive your congratulations and good wishes. By looking back thirty-one years we may see how much can be done from small beginnings. I have spoken of the commencement of this society before, but I will refer to it again to-night. I knew of but one conference in this country, and that was in St. Peter's Parish, New York. Knowing the pastor I visited him and got from him a full explanation of the workings of the society. I then determined to establish a conference in Boston and remembered the advice, "first look out for a good president." This we found in Mr. James Collins, who I am sorry to see is not here to-night.

If you wish to be true brothers of St. Vincent, there are some things which you must remember. By doing good to the poor you do good to yourselves. You bring to the poor on your missions hearts filled with the love of God, and you want their hearts to be filled with the love of God also. If the poor have neglected their faith, it is your duty to bring them back to religion. A word from you will have a great effect on the poor whom you visit.

I am glad to hear from the report the good percentage of attendance at the meetings. When the attendance is good, we can be assured that the poor are being well cared for. I am glad to see these new Conferences. I am glad to see the colored Conference, and the Conference of the young men. Young blood is good for you, good for the society, and and the society is good for the young men themselves. I have received many addresses and congratulations, but none have touched me more than this meeting tonight.

After advising the members to persevere in their good work, and assuring them of his continued interest and support, His Grace concluded by giving his blessing to all present.

The address read by President Ring for the society was artistically engraved on card board and set in a beautiful silver frame.

CARMELITE NUNS.

This memorial volume would be incomplete without some reference to the Carmelite Nuns, a branch of whose order was established in Boston, August 27, 1890, the centennial anniversary of their arrival in America. After getting permission from Archbishop Williams, a few Catholic gentlemen, whose attention was particularly attracted to the order while attending the Catholic Convention in Baltimore in 1889, leased a suitable house in Roxbury, corner of Centre and Cedar streets, and placed it at the disposal of the Reverend Superior. Five Sisters are now located here, secluded from the world in person, but united with it in spirit, their lives being wholly devoted to praying for the people at large.

The following extract from a letter written by a lady, gives an interesting account of a visit recently made to the nunnery here, accompanied by a friend : —

It was a bright, sunny afternoon in April, when we found an opportunity of making a visit, planned for some months, to the newly established Carmelites in Roxbury. Arriving at the place to which we had been directed, there was no mistaking the embryo monastery; an air of as perfect seclusion as an ordinary old-fashioned dwelling house would admit, led us at once to the door bearing a sign, "Walk in, and ring at the Turn." We entered, closed two doors, behind us and found ourselves confronted by a wall with a circular projection bearing a resemblance to a sentry-box. At the side hung a handle attached to a long chain. A door was on the right and one on the left. All was perfect silence. We stood a moment uncertain and somewhat awed by — we knew not what; then, smiling at our own embarrassment, pulled the handle. A bell rang somewhere inside, and the next moment there was a rustle and a soft voice was heard asking what we wished. Startled, we looked around —

no one to be seen — nothing to be seen — but what has been described. Again came the question, and one of us plucked up courage to advance nearer, and seeing then an opening between the "Turn" and the wall, told who we were and asked to see Sister Augustine.

"Yes; step into the speak-room, on your right, please."

We opened the door as directed and entered a small room having a door opposite the one by which we had come in and partitioned off the left by a wooden lattice; eight or ten inches behind it was another partition of wooden rails, and behind that a black curtain. All was silence. There were two chairs beside the lattice, and we seated ourselves in these, looking timidly at one another and almost afraid to speak. Then came the rustle again, the sound of quick, light steps, the little rattling, tinkling of rosary beads, and we were welcomed in cordial tones.

"We are glad to have people come," they said; "not that we would want visitors all the time, but in coming to a new place it is pleasant to meet some friends."

With one exception, Boston is an entirely strange place for all the Sisters.

The greeting over, we learned that one of the sisters present, Sister Gertrude, was a daughter of the late Mr. McMasters of the *Freeman's Journal*. As one of us had been reading the Life of Father Hecker in the *Catholic World*, in which Mr. McMasters is mentioned, we asked if it were the same. Sister told us that it was, and gave us some of the details of his life, mentioning that there were three of the family now leading a religious life — "Three vocations instead of one."

As we had not met Sister Augustine (Miss Eulalie Tuckerman, in the world) since she joined the Sisterhood, we had many questions to ask and answer, and the time sped quickly. Occasionally the bell rang, and Sister Augustine, being "Turn Sister," would excuse herself, to return in a few minutes and resume conversation. Once or twice Sister Gertrude, too, left us to consult Reverend Mother on some matter in which we were interested. The light, quick, springing footsteps seemed to blend with, rather than break, the quietness of the place.

All too soon was the visit over, and begging the prayers of these hidden holy souls, we said goodbye. A generous friend had given us a box of flowers for the nuns, on learning our destination, so we were initiated into the mysteries of the "Turn." The circular projection we had noticed was turned and disclosed a cupboard with two shelves; putting the box on, we got the key and made a short visit to the lowly little chapel, the centre and secret of the peace and quiet of the house — the grated door near the altar, the sweet voices of the nuns heard for a minute chanting, was all that distinguished it from any other oratory.

As we returned the key to the "Turn," we heard again the low voice of Sister Augustine telling us to take some pictures she had laid on the shelf for us, and making our final adieux and promising to come again, the "Turn" closed and we went slowly out, feeling that much good must come to Boston from the presence of such a community.

M. B. C.

THE STUDENTS' GIFT.

On Saturday, March 7, feast of St. Thomas Aquinas, the students of St. John's Seminary, Brighton, gave Archbishop Williams an entertainment in honor of his silver jubilee. It consisted of a theological disputation, essays and music. It was followed by the presentation to the Archbishop of the students' gift — a magnificent Pontificale Romanum and Canon Missae. These came from Paris, and are the best style of the bookmakers' art. The Archbishop made appropriate response, assuring the students of the happiness it will be to him to use their noble gift when conferring Holy Orders on themselves.

A CARD.

The Catholic Union of Boston has ordered that its grateful acknowledgments be publicly made, thanking all who assisted its committee on the occasion of its Silver Jubilee Reception to Most Rev. John J. Williams, D. D., at Boston College Hall, March 12, especially Rev. Edward I. Devitt, S. J., president, and his reverend assistants of Boston College, Brother T. J. Fealy, S. J., the Young Men's Catholic Association of Boston College, Mrs. Mary Elizabeth Blake, Hon. Thomas J. Gargan, Mr. Thomas A. Mullen, Mr. John C. Mullaly, the ladies and gentlemen who formed the bouquet of artists, Mr. J. Frank Donahoe, Mr. James T. Whelan, Mr. Stephen O'Meara of the *Journal*, Mr. Bernard Corr, Mr. John M. Crowley, Mr. Joseph H. Sheehan, Thomas O'Callaghan & Co., and the press for most generous notices before and after the reception.

THOMAS B. FITZ, *President*.

JOHN J. McCLUSKEY, *Rec. Sec. and Treas*.

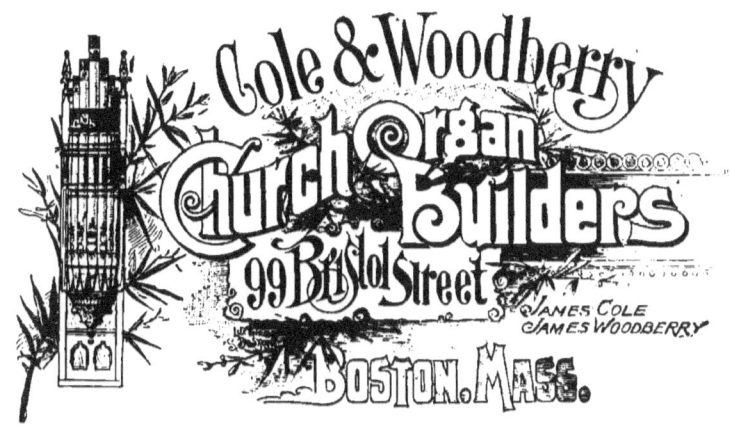

SPECIFICATIONS AND ESTIMATES FOR NEW
ORGANS OF ALL SIZES, ALSO FOR THE
RE-BUILDING, RENOVATING AND
ENLARGEMENT OF ORGANS.

Tuning and Repairing by First-Class Workmen.

DESCRIPTIVE CATALOGUES AND TESTIMONIALS MAILED FREE.

FLYNN & MAHONY,

Nos. 18 & 20 ESSEX STREET, - - - BOSTON,
NEAR WASHINGTON STREET.

CATHOLIC PUBLISHERS,

Church Goods and Religious Articles,

PRAYER-BOOKS, ROSARIES, STATUES,
——:AND:——
RELIGIOUS PICTURES,
Framed and Unframed.
Gold and Silver Medals, Candelabra, Candlesticks, Etc.
THE BEST AND MOST COMPLETE LINE OF RELIGIOUS
GOODS IN NEW ENGLAND.

UPTOWN AGENTS FOR ALL THE STEAMSHIP LINES:
CUNARD LINE, INMAN LINE, ANCHOR LINE, ALLAN LINE,
GUION LINE, WARREN LINE, WHITE STAR LINE.

CABIN, INTERMEDIATE AND STEERAGE PASSAGE TICKETS
AT LOW RATES.

ESTABLISHED IN 1849.

FINEST TONE, BEST WORK AND MATERIAL.

PIANOS

PRICES MODERATE AND TERMS REASONABLE.

50,000 MADE AND IN USE.

EVERY INSTRUMENT FULLY WARRANTED.

ILLUSTRATED CATALOGUE FREE.

EMERSON PIANO CO.

174 TREMONT STREET, BOSTON, MASS.

92 FIFTH AVENUE, NEW YORK.

THESE instruments have enjoyed a high reputation for more than forty years. Are **Brilliant and Musical in tone,** and afford a most beautiful accompaniment to vocal music—the tone having that rare **sympathetic quality** which blends admirably with the **human voice.** They are **Durable,** being constructed of the **Best Materials,** by the **Most Skillful Workmen.** They have earned an especial reputation for **Keeping in Tune,** and also for retaining in a most remarkable degree their original fullness of tone—never growing thin or wiry with age.

The **Emerson Upright Pianos** especially have obtained a remarkable success during the past few years, and have invariably received the highest award wherever exhibited. In all the essential qualities of a

FIRST-CLASS INSTRUMENT

they are not surpassed by any Pianos manufactured in the country. Do not fail to investigate the merits of these Pianos before purchasing. It will repay you.

Superior Pianos to Rent. Old Pianos taken in exchange. Pianos tuned and repaired.

Factory - - - - *No. 520 Harrison Avenue,*

BOSTON, MASS.

PATRICK H. POWERS,
ORRIN A. KIMBALL, } PROPRIETORS.
JOSEPH GRAMER,

McDONNELL AND SONS,
QUARRY OWNERS, QUINCY, MASS.

Branch Office and Yard, 858 & 860 Main St., Buffalo, N. Y.

ESTABLISHED IN 1857.

We have reached that point in our business where we can refer with pride to many of the prominent monuments in this country. We have our own quarry, polishing mill, teams, etc., and, being situated in this favorable position, have a decided advantage over competitors in speedy execution of orders entrusted to us, the guarantee of perfect stock, and in quoting close estimates. We furnish all the leading granites, in addition to our celebrated Quincy granite. We have in our employ an experienced monumental draughtsman, and under his personal supervision, we are enabled to submit drawings and plans perfectly proportioned, original in design, etc. We have made a study of proportions, one of the most essential features of a monument. Giving us an opportunity of competing on your work will cost you nothing, will probably save you money, and, above all, give you a satisfactory monument. We have a large collection of new designs from which to form an idea of what you desire.

QUINCY GRANITE,

LIGHT, MEDIUM AND DARK; ROUGH AND DRESSED.

THEIS & JANSSEN,

Ecclesiastical * and * Architectural * Marble * Works,

CARVERS IN MARBLE AND STONE,

413 & 415 East 25th Street, - - NEW YORK.

JOSEPH SIBBEL,
Modeller AND **Sculptor,**
STUDIO, 214 EAST 26th ST.,
NEW YORK.

NICHOLAS M. WILLIAMS,

(SEXTON OF THE CATHEDRAL,)

FUNERAL DIRECTOR

AND

FURNISHING

UNDERTAKER,

1386 WASHINGTON STREET,

Near the Cathedral.   **BOSTON.**

Competent men in attendance at all hours of the day and night.

During the day, call at the store; and by night, ring the night bell on Union Park Street.

Royal Bavarian Art Establishment.

MAYER & CO.,
OF
MUNICH, LONDON, NEW YORK.

◅STAINED GLASS.▻
MAYER'S FAMOUS MUNICH
STATUES, STATIONS OF THE CROSS, Etc.

We beg to mention a few Churches where specimens of our Stained Glass may be seen:
ST. MARY'S CHURCH, Charlestown, Boston, Mass.

NEW YORK CITY.

St. Stephen's Church, E. 28th St.	Church of the Assumption, W. 49th St.
St. John the Evangelist. E. 55th St.	Library, Columbia College, E. 49th St.
St. Gabriel's Church, E. 37th St.	Chapel of the Sacred Heart Convent, Manhattanville.
St. Mary's Church, Grand St.	
Church of the Paulist Fathers, W. 59th Street.	St. Agnes' Church, Hoyt and Sackett Sts., Brooklyn.

New York Branch, 124 **WEST 23d STREET.**

Established 1863.   Continuation of a House Established 1840.

PRICE LISTS
OF
PURE ALTAR WINES
AND GENERAL VARIETY ON APPLICATION.

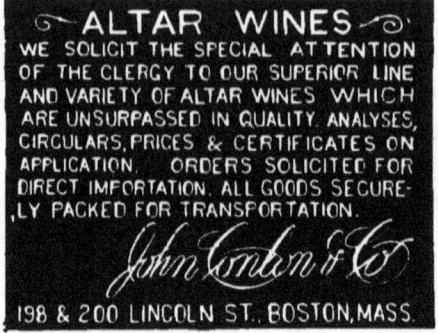

— SPECIALTIES —

FINEST GRADES OF OLD AND CHOICE GOODS
FOR FAMILY USE AND SICKNESS, IN WOOD AND GLASS.

Samples Forwarded by Mail when Desired.

A. ERTLE,
164 Prince St., New York City.

Church + Decorator.

Interior Decorations
AND
Fresco Painting,

For Buildings of every character, in any of the classics, adapted to new and original designs.

Ecclesiastical Work of the Highest order.
ALTAR PIECES,
Emblematical and Allegorical Characters and Figures for Churches, Stations, and Banners

POLYCHROMATIC DECORATING
In Color and Gilding, for High Altars.
Church Banners to Order Artistically Executed.
None but first-class Artists employed,
And all work guaranteed.

Among the many churches I have done of late, I refer to Church of the Immaculate Conception, E. 14th St., N. Y.; St. Mary's, Grand St , New York; Church of St. John Evangelist, E. 55th St. and First Ave., N. Y ; St. Bridget's Church, Ave. B., N. Y. City; Chapel of the Redemptorist Fathers, South Fifth Ave , N. Y. City; Church of the Holy Name of Jesus, Chicopee, Mass,; St. Mary's Church, Auburn, N. Y.; St. Patrick's Church, West Troy, N. Y.; Cathedral of St. Paul, Pittsburgh, Pa,; St. Mary's Church, Fall River, Mass.

UNION INSTITUTION FOR SAVINGS
IN THE CITY OF BOSTON,

590 WASHINGTON STREET,
CORNER HAYWARD PLACE.

Incorporated   - - -   1865.

Deposits,	- - -	$3,912,578
Surplus,	- - -	$163,051

Always paid a semi-annual dividend.
Deposits from $3 to $1000 placed on interest second Wednesdays of November, February, May and August.

HUGH O'BRIEN,
President.

WM. S. PELLETIER,
Treasurer.

JAMES L CORR & CO.,
PRINTERS
AND
CATHOLIC PUBLISHERS,
286 WASHINGTON STREET,
OPP SCHOOL ST.   BOSTON.
TELEPHONE 2257.

CHURCH AND SOCIETY PRINTING
OF ALL KINDS.

www.ingramcontent.com/pod-product-compliance
Lightning Source LLC
Chambersburg PA
CBHW030256170426
43202CB00009B/773